# DREAM SYMBOL WORK

## Unlocking the Energy
## from Dreams and Spiritual Experiences

### PATRICIA H. BERNE AND LOUIS M. SAVARY

*Paulist Press • New York*

Library of Congress Cataloging-in-Publication Data

Berne, Patricia H.
     Dream symbol work: Unlocking the Energy from Dreams and Spiritual Experiences/
     Patricia H. Berne and Louis M. Savary.
         p.  cm.
     Includes bibliographical references.
     ISBN 0–8091–3219–2
     1. Dreams.   2. Symbolism (Psychology).   3. Spiritual life.   I. Savary, Louis M.
     II. Title.
     BF1078.B438       1991
     154.6'3—dc20                                                          90-27749
                                                                              CIP

Published by Paulist Press
997 Macarthur Boulevard
Mahwah, New Jersey 07430

Printed and bound in the
United States of America

# CONTENTS

*PART II*
SPIRITUALITY AND DREAMS

*PART III*
THE SYMBOL TECHNIQUES

# INTRODUCTION

Throughout history the symbol has been an integral element of human civilization: the olive branch, the sword, the Olympic flame, the dragon, the snake, the star, the cross, the bell, the banner, the sacred book, the oath, the table, the tomb. In religion, politics, warfare, sports, business, art, literature, architecture, oratory, music and fashion, the symbol is what we tend to remember: the altar, the siren, the gavel, the bugle call, the trophy, the uniform, the flag, the stethoscope. Life is filled with symbols and images, all charged with meanings and emotions, and therefore with energy.

In many ways, the past decade has witnessed the rediscovery of the power of symbols and images. In education, right-brain learning has used intuition, affective expression, and nonlinear imaginative thinking to break the old molds of traditional pedagogy. Industrial trainers, workshop leaders, religious evangelists, and political candidates have joined a renaissance of communicating through story and image. Madison Avenue advertising experts who created McDonald's Golden Arches, the Marlboro Man, the AT&T logo, the MGM lion, *The New York Times* masthead and designer labels, continually refine their symbol-making techniques in a marketplace where millions of vendors pitch their products twenty-four hours a day. Theoreticians of the creative process who want to help you create new jobs, new relationships and even new selves, agree on one thing: imaging and symbolizing the result you want is an essential element for success. Meditators of all faiths and fads use visualization of symbols to heighten the intensity of their spiritual practices. Many psychotherapists have integrated innovative uses of symbolic imagery into their traditional clinical practices in the techniques of guided imagery and hypnotherapy. Cancer researcher O. Carl Simonton, M.D., had patients visualize healthy cells conquering and destroying the cancer cells in their bodies. Cancer surgeon Bernie Siegel, M.D., has patients use crayons to draw pictures

1

of themselves in hopes of revealing a possible path to healing and wholeness.

Symbols and images permeate our lives. Each of us has our own favorite symbols. Which ones are yours? The butterfly? The rose? The cat? The pearl? Your car? If symbols are a major part of our waking life, they are much more so a major part of our dream life. As noted by C.G. Jung and others, symbols are the language of dreams.

Central to the study of dreams, interest in which has grown steadily over the past 20 years, is the exploration of the symbols, figures, and images in dreams. Many dreamers claim that their dreams fade quickly upon awakening, except for an image or symbol which may stubbornly linger throughout the day, or even longer. The power latent in a dream symbol is indicated by its refusal to disappear into one's "lost and forgotten" memory banks. Such a symbol is laden with energy. When worked with properly, it can be a veritable mine of personal, emotional, cognitive, and spiritual resources. Everyone knows that when a dream is vividly recalled, the elements of the dream which evoke the most meaning and power are its symbols.

Symbols from dreams and waking life have energy and wisdom for us. Their potential waits to be dug out and used to empower our daily actions and choices.

In an earlier book, *Dreams and Spiritual Growth,* we presented a comprehensive, practical approach for dealing with dream material as a source for holistic growth. Among that book's more than thirty-seven dreamwork techniques, we presented five specifically helpful in working with symbols. In this book we have refined those five and added another dozen, providing a large variety of practical techniques that are especially helpful and effective in exploring your symbols. In that earlier book, we also introduced the idea of symbols as bearers of energy.

## SYMBOLS AND ENERGY

For the physicist, energy is defined as "the ability to do work"—physical work, of course. As technicians of the spiritual, we apply the term "energy" analogously in the psychological and spiritual domains. Thus, psychological energy is the ability to do psychological work, such as reasoning, analyzing, describing, and communicating. Spiritual energy, which operates in the domain of the human spirit, is the ability to do spiritual work, such as creating, forgiving, believing, discerning, transmitting life, affirming oneself, showing compassion, giving meaning to things, making commitments.

In this book we focus on the symbol as a user-friendly container of energy, available for personal growth. You are accustomed to dealing with containers of physical energy designed for human use. Electrical power lines contain energy and bring it safely into your house. Your auto's fuel tank is a container and bearer of energy that enables you to travel. The wood in your fireplace is a container of energy that enables you to conveniently heat your home. The container aspect of energy is important, because that's what makes the energy available to you and ready for use. A sky full of lightning is uncontained energy, oil bursting from a ruptured tanker is uncontained energy, a forest of trees is not a convenient source of energy if you want a fire in your fireplace tonight. The best way for humans to deal with energy is in a container, because a container can be borne from place to place, it can be used when needed, as much as is needed, and the rest stored. In this sense, symbols are very useful containers and bearers of energy. In this book we suggest ways to utilize these symbol-energies on a daily basis in order to live your life more fully, enjoyably, and holistically.

Symbol work is defined as the application of symbol techniques to clarify and evoke the conscious and unconscious psychological and spiritual energies contained in your symbols. Symbol work is not primarily analyzing, explaining, or interpreting the symbol. We emphasize the importance and wisdom of staying with the symbol itself, working and interacting with it, until you are able to release, use, and develop the energy it contains.

We do believe it is an incomplete use of a symbol merely to interpret it and stop there. The Christian cross, for example, isn't meant just to be analyzed and intellectually understood, but rather is to be treated as a container or channel of energy. To give or find a symbol's meaning is to release energy. To give meaning releases, for example, the energy to make choices, to discriminate and discern, to see relationships, or to act wisely. A symbol, moreover, usually does not have a single meaning but rather a cluster of meanings.

Similarly, a symbol usually does not release a single energy, but a complex of energies. Even when you identify a dream symbol as releasing, say, heroic energy, the heroic really represents a constellation of different energies, such as the ability to take risks, do great deeds, be a pioneer, confront danger and fear, take aggressive action when necessary, activities traditionally associated with the term "hero."

What is unique about the energy contained in a symbol, especially one from the collective unconscious, is that its energy resources are continually renewed and ever-available. A symbol may have one level of meaning in your present life, but it remains a dynamic force throughout your life, revealing other levels of energy as you need them. In this book, we explore a mask symbol and see how it provides a continuing source of energy for the dreamer. As she said, "I can probably continue to tap into the energy released by the mask for the rest of my life. I can see how it applies right now, and as long as I continue to deal with the roles I have to play in life, and the different masks I wear, I can see the symbol, for years, bringing me wisdom and insight to make important choices."

## WAKING LIFE SYMBOLS

Energy is contained in all symbols and symbolic events, not just in symbols from your dreams.

Even people who don't remember their dreams can identify their favorite symbols, symbolic objects, or symbolic events. You probably know people who are fascinated with parrots, daisies, rainbows, candles, crystals, Depression glassware, Agatha Christie mysteries, antique autos, jazz recordings, classic clothing, leather boots, Jacobean furniture, or something else.

We know a woman who collects butterfly things: earrings, brooches, blouses, photos, paintings, address labels, stamps, stories, anything that has the image of a butterfly on it or is about butterflies. Even when she doodles, she draws butterflies. When a monarch flits by her kitchen window, she stops whatever she's doing and watches it—even talks to it. For her, anything connected with butterflies releases a certain energy. "Butterflies remind me of the gift of life," she explained, "the gift of freedom, and God's love for me. So, whenever I see a butterfly, I feel loved, free, and alive."

For others, their most powerful symbols may be a certain song they find themselves humming and whistling, a poem whose images keep surfacing, a saying they frequently repeat, a place to which they keep wanting to return, a person who keeps coming to mind, a relationship that generates strong feelings, a time of day (sunrise, sunset), a certain kind of weather, a certain special season of the year, a favorite smell or scent.

Do you find yourself attracted to a certain character in the comic strips? Do you happen to like one particular television commercial? Is there a certain character from a soap opera that you hate? Or love? Does a certain corporate slogan anger you? Do you have a certain favorite work of art? Do you have a favorite saint or biblical character? Do you look for certain images when you buy greeting cards? Such symbolic persons, places, things, or events may be worked with in the same way as dream symbols.

Religious symbols, for example, such as icons, crucifixes, statues, altars, pulpits, steeples, bells, chants, vestments, and rituals, are designed to release religious energies; artistic symbols, such as lines, colors, shapes, textures, forms, sounds, rhythms, and the like, are designed to release aesthetic energies; commercial symbols, such as product labels, theme songs, mottos, celebrity endorsements, attractive models, and so on, are designed to get people to buy the product behind the symbol.

Just as advertisers research the energies released by different symbols, so you can do symbol work with your personal symbols, in order to release energy for your own personal growth and development.

STRUCTURE

*Dream Symbol Work,* divided into three parts, is designed both for reading enjoyment and practical how-to help. Part III contains technical descriptions of the symbol techniques we present and explains how to use each one step-by-step. Thus, if you would immediately like to explore a powerful symbol from your dream or from some moment in your life, you may go directly to Part III, which provides the structural bones and muscles of the book.

Part I, the flesh and blood of the book, explores in great detail a major dream, "The Child in the Golden Mask," that Patricia Berne had over a dozen years ago and with which she has been doing symbol work since then. In Part I, she takes you through her own personal journey using all of the symbol techniques, allowing you to experience an actual dreamer using an actual dream and watch its powerful symbols releasing their meaning and energy in her life.

Not only is it a fascinating story, but it gives life to the techniques. Parts I and III of the book follow parallel paths.

Part II presents our theory about dreams and spirituality, and offers a rationale for doing symbol work as a spiritual practice.

For us, spirituality may be defined as "my way of living, acting, and choosing in light of my ultimate values." Thus, spirituality has to do with both "ultimate" things and "everyday" things and how the two classes of actions are integrated. Effective symbol work not only reveals your conscious and unconscious ultimate values, but also suggests ways to enrich your daily life through conscious choices, using the energies that may be released from the symbols in your dreams and your life.

## Part I

# Symbol Work on the Dream of the Child in the Golden Mask

# Chapter 1

# THE DREAM OF THE CHILD IN THE GOLDEN MASK

## INTRODUCTION TO THE MASK DREAM EXPERIENCE (TOLD BY THE DREAMER)

About twelve years ago, I was part of a group of about forty Ph.D. candidates from a variety of fields who had been brought together for a month of interaction and interdisciplinary sharing. We were to live together, get to know each other, and learn from each other. I had been at the colloquium for only a few days and did not know who was who yet, though we had all introduced ourselves the first night.

In between scheduled programs that morning, I had wandered out to the swimming pool area. A young woman was there reading. When I sat down next to her she looked up and, apparently remembering that I had introduced myself as a mother at the opening of the colloquium, asked me whether or not I thought it was really important for a woman to have children.

I didn't answer her question directly, which was unusual for me since I generally take any available opportunity to talk about my children. Instead, I said, "That reminds me that I had a dream last night in which I discovered that I had given birth to twins."

Though I didn't realize it at the time, this woman happened to be the one person in the group who specialized in researching dreams. In fact, she was currently collecting dreams for an anthology of women's dreams reflecting cultural issues. So, she asked me to tell her my dream.

When two or more events that are not causally connected happen at the same time and place and affect the destiny of one or more people, it is called "synchronicity." I wasn't familiar with the term then, but that encounter with her at the pool certainly proved an experience of it for me.

I don't know if she suggested closing my eyes and reexperiencing the dream, or if I just did it spontaneously. (It's what I now often

9

ask my clients to do when they tell me a dream.) But, with eyes closed, I went back into the experience of the dream in a sort of contemplative or meditative way. In the telling, I reexperienced the dream with much emotion. I must have been very deeply into the experience, because I never noticed that about twenty others of our group had gathered and were silently listening to my dream.

Here is the dream as I then wrote it down.

### The Dream of the Child in the Golden Mask

*DREAM REPORT*

> *January, 1976*
> *St. Petersburg, Florida*
> *Colloquium*

*I am in my house and hear a baby crying. I go upstairs into a small nursery room to look at the child in the crib. The room is all white, the crib is cream-colored and its front panel holds a decal of a bunny in pink. The sides of the crib are up and there is a small baby girl in the crib. She is sleeping soundly. She has dark curly hair, and her dark eyelashes are touching her round, rosy cheeks. I stand admiring her and think how she is so very fair, sweet and good, so beautiful and peaceful. She is lying on her stomach with her knees drawn up under her, her bottom in the air. And she has on pink ruffled panties over her diaper. She looks like such a darling little girl. I stand there looking at her, delighting in her sweetness and thinking what a good little girl she is.*

*But I realize I am still hearing the loud crying sounds, the awful plaintive wails of a hungry and desperately-in-need child. I am confused. Here before me in her crib is my child and she is asleep. But the crying still persists.*

*I see a door at the end of the nursery that I had not noticed before. I walk over, open it, and step into a room exactly like the nursery. Same dimensions, color, and crib. There is even the same bunny decal on the panel of the crib. In this crib is a child of exactly the same size and age* as the good little girl, except I cannot see the child's face or head, for the head is totally encased in a golden mask. A shiny, yellow-gold mask, very smooth and beautiful, in the style of the artist Henry Moore, very simple and exquisite in its simplicity.

This is the crying child.

I pick up the child to comfort it and, through the terrycloth, stretch pajamas it is wearing, I can feel that its body is emaciated, undernourished. I very much want to feed this child, but realize the mask is made so that there is no open mouth-space. The mask does have a slight opening for each nostril so the child can breathe. There are also tiny, elliptical eye-spaces in the mask for the eyes, and if I look deeply into them I can see the beseeching, desperate look in these, my baby's eyes. I am very sad.

I cannot understand how I could have forgotten that I had two babies. How did I forget that I gave birth to this second child at the same time I gave birth to the beautiful, well-nourished child in the next room? I feel so bad. I tell myself it had been a forgetting, not a rejection, of the child in the golden mask. I just didn't know I had both to care for.

I try to get the mask off so I can nurse the crying child. There is no opening in the metal, no latch or hinge. It is a solid, encasing piece of gold, terribly strong. I try fitting my fingers under it at the throat and hope to slip it off. That doesn't work, for the mask is made exactly to the head's contour—like a death mask of gold. I think, "Maybe I can use a can opener to cut through the metal." I rush to get a can opener, the old-fashioned kind with a sharp, open blade. But I can see, as I go to use it, that I could accidentally hurt or even mortally injure the child. My anxiety grows.

I begin to panic. Then I realize I need to be calm and think, to analyze the situation logically and find a solution.

With all my effort, I force myself to be calm, to comfort this crying, starving child in the gold mask. I try to focus my concentration, to think of what else I might be able to do to get the mask off. To find a way to feed the child while the mask is still on, I realize, is not a long-term solution. The head will continue to grow, while the mask cannot grow, and so the child's head will be distorted and its brain finally crushed. The child cannot grow with the mask in place.

I calm the child to just a whimper using the warmth of my body and my voice for comfort.

I begin to force myself to think about the problem as calmly and rationally as I can. Finally, I realize that it's possible to go to a professional. A jeweler who works in gold and other precious metals would have the unique tools and professional skills to remove the mask without mortally injuring the child. I put the child back in its crib and go downstairs to the phone. I open the telephone's Yellow Pages and look under "Jewelers" for a goldsmith. I find one and call him. He answers, and I tell him what I need him to do. He does not seem surprised or ask any questions. He says he will be there as soon as possible. I go upstairs to comfort the child and try to control my anxiety while I wait for the goldsmith to come and remove the golden mask.

## Chapter 2

# SYMBOL WORK—AWARENESS TECHNIQUES

Here is a dreamer with a dream report. The golden mask dream is an important dream, perhaps a major dream in her life. What can she do with it? What does it mean? What is it saying to her? What is it asking of her? How does she begin to unravel it? To make sense of it?

The dream is filled with powerful symbols. Perhaps they hold the key to the dream? How to begin? What symbol should she work on first?

When she first told the dream to the woman by the pool in Florida, almost twenty people had gathered around to hear the telling of it.

"This was my first experience of a dreamsharing/dreamwork group," she reported, "as it was for most of the others. And when I finished telling my dream and opened my eyes, they began asking me questions the way a good dreamwork group would. That helped me process the dream material so that I could begin to find and release the dream's energy."

Many who listened were impressed at a deep level by her telling of the dream and the discussion that followed, because in the following days some of them began to report having mask dreams of their own as well as dreams reflecting other symbols in her dream. In this way, her dream also became a dream for the community.

Although she did a number of general dreamwork techniques, her specific work with the dream symbols turned out to be the most productive. The group's questions elicited from her much of the same information that, in a more structured way, can be gotten by using the first eight dream symbol techniques presented in this book. The rest of this section describes her working through sixteen symbol techniques.

Although her lengthy symbol work might seem overwhelming to you, remember that she completed it over a period of time, actually a number of years. You may not want to do so thorough a job on your symbols, and that's all right. For her, this dream was a major dream and a turning point in her life and destiny. It deserved all the work she put into it, and the fruits of her labors were plentiful. Also, once she began working on the dream it released energy for additional dreamwork. The dream became a touchstone of comfort, support, and guidance for her.

As she relives her symbol work for you, let yourself get imaginatively involved in her experience, so that when you begin to work with your own symbols, the process will feel familiar.

## INTRODUCTORY TECHNIQUE: MAKE A DREAM REPORT

No matter what kind of dreamwork you are doing, begin by writing out a dream report; that is, capture in words the dream as you recall it, the way it happened, in all its details. A dream report is very valuable because it is the raw material upon which all other dreamwork is based. You will return to it again and again.

In the dream report, include the events of the dream in the order in which they occurred. Describe the figures and symbols in the dream in terms of their size, shape, color, age, and other special features; for example, if they are familiar or strange, old or new, and especially if they are different from normal in any way.

In her dream report, the woman noted that the second, duplicate nursery was a surprise because she had never noticed it before. The second child was also a surprise, and the mask on its head made it strikingly unusual. She also compared the two infants in some detail, and that comparison, contained in the dream report, would prove to be significant once she began doing symbol work.

At each step along the way in the dream, she also reported her feelings and those of the two children. The affective components of a dream are important and should find their place in the dream report.

Much can be learned about a dream simply by writing a dream report. When asked what she had learned from putting her dream into words on paper, this is how the dreamer replied:

*What did I learn from writing out my dream? As I look at the words I have written I can see the paradox. The adjectives describing the good, fair, beautiful child reflect so much of the me I strive to be. The adjectives that describe the child in the mask show it as forgotten, angry, wailing, under-*

*nourished, dying and beseeching, needing to be freed of a beautiful, valuable (since it is gold) mask. I get a sense of the tension, the urgency, the conflict. I am comforted that, with the imminent arrival of the goldsmith, the dream hints at a resolution and offers symbolic guidance. It points in a direction.*

This technique, as well as a number of others for working with dreams in general, may be found in our earlier book, *Dreams and Spiritual Growth* (Paulist, 1984). The following techniques in the present book all focus specifically on symbols, whether they occur in dreams or daily life.

### TECHNIQUE 1: IDENTIFY SYMBOLS IN A DREAM REPORT

To begin doing symbol work, it is best to survey the dream in question and take note of its symbols. The simplest way to do this is to reread your dream report and *underline the symbols that seem clear and vivid.* Technique 1 is simple and takes only a minute or two to complete. In doing it you generate, as it were, a symbol menu. Technique 2 will tell you how to select from your menu.

The dreamer underlined the following symbols from her dream, the ones that seemed most vivid to her and those she thought might merit symbol work.

*Good and sweet baby girl*
*Crib with bunny decal*
*Door to second nursery*
*Angry, hungry child (in golden mask)*
*Golden mask*
*Old fashioned can opener*
*Telephone's Yellow Pages*
*Goldsmith*

"In the months and years after the dream," she reported, "I worked on each of those symbols and learned a lot about myself."

But, for this book, she chose one symbol and focused on it, to demonstrate how all the techniques work. Technique 2 shows how she selected the first symbol.

## TECHNIQUE 2: CHOOSE A SYMBOL ON WHICH TO FOCUS

This technique allows you to answer the question: *What symbol do I want to work on at this time?* It helps you sort out which symbols generate the most interest and emotional intensity for you, and it invites you to rank the symbols in their present order of importance.

To do this technique, the dreamer first made a list of all the symbols she underlined in her dream report.

Next, considering each symbol in turn, she asked herself: "Am I attracted toward this symbol, repulsed by it, or do I feel neutral toward it?" After symbols to which she was attracted, she drew an arrow aiming toward the symbol (←). If she felt repulsed, the arrow went the other way (→). As for the golden mask itself, she was both attracted and repulsed, which she indicated by two arrows (← →). She put a zero (0) next to the Telephone's Yellow Pages and Door to Second Nursery, since they evoked neither attraction nor repulsion.

Next, since not all symbols exert the same power, she then marked with an asterisk (*) those symbols that produced the most powerful effect on her.

Finally, she was able to rank the symbols in the order she wanted to work on them.

This is how her Technique 2 symbol work looked when she finished:

*Most powerful symbols:*

1. *Golden mask* ← → *
2. *Angry, hungry child (in golden mask)* ← *
3. *Sweet, good baby girl* ← *
4. *Goldsmith* ←
5. *Old fashioned can opener* →
6. *Door to second nursery* 0
7. *Telephone's Yellow Pages* 0

You may recall that in the dream itself, she expressed strong emotions toward the *child* in the golden mask. Yet, in the process of doing this symbol technique it became clear to her that the golden mask itself was the symbol that would unlock the first major meaning for her. As in the dream, she felt the mask needed to be dealt with first in order to get to the child. For her, too, the mask had the double energy of attraction and repulsion, possibly a clue to its special power.

We usually conclude each symbol technique by asking the dreamer: "What did you learn from doing this technique?"

The dreamer of the golden mask replied:

*I guess I knew intuitively that the golden mask would be the key that would unlock the meaning and purpose of the entire dream. So, I decided to do major symbol work on it. The mask both contained the child and was the barrier to seeing the child. I knew I had to deal with the mask before I could be free to work directly with the symbol of the child. I felt very concerned about the child that was suffering inside the mask, but I felt it was more important, first, to discover what that mask symbolized. Why was that mask there?*

*I had known of the work of Carl Gustav Jung for some years and had heard lecturers apply his symbolism to art and literature, but I had not yet learned to apply it to my dreams. If, at the time of the mask dream, I had known how, I perhaps would have simply categorized the dream as a persona dream, and not have been so moved by it. Instead, the mask symbol felt new and powerful to me. I was sure it held special insight and wisdom for me. I needed to immerse myself in it.*

## TECHNIQUE 3: GET IMMERSED IN THE SYMBOL

This immersion technique is essential when you are working with a dreamwork partner, counselor, therapist, or in a dream group. Doing this technique together guarantees that the symbol in the minds and imaginations of the others is the same in all its details as the symbol experienced by the dreamer. In doing dreamwork with others, it may be confusing to the dreamer if the others have an image of the symbol quite different from that which the dreamer has. When the partners' image of the symbol is close to that of the dreamer, partners can be helpful with their questions and on-target with their input.

Most importantly, however, this technique helps the dreamer

see the symbol more clearly and relate to it more effectively. For the dreamer, the immersion questions heighten the awareness of the symbol, begin building a relationship to the symbol, clarify its details, and often produce insights and metaphoric statements about the symbol's meaning and energy.

In doing symbol work with the golden mask, the dreamer might have been tempted to omit the immersion technique, since this symbol was remarkably well-described in the dream report:

> *I cannot see the child's face or head, for the head is totally encased in a golden mask. A shiny, yellow-gold mask, very smooth and beautiful, in the style of the artist Henry Moore, very simple and exquisite in its simplicity.*

> *. . . the mask is made so that there is no open mouth-space. The mask does have a slight opening for each nostril so the child can breathe. There are also tiny, elliptical spaces in the mask for the eyes, and if I look deeply into them I can see . . . my baby's eyes.*

> *There is no opening place in the metal, no latch or hinge. It is a solid, encasing piece of gold, terribly strong. I try fitting my fingers under it at the throat and hope to slip it off. That doesn't work, for the mask is made exactly to the head's contour . . .*

Despite the many specific facts that the dreamer does provide in the dream report, other questions about the description of the mask still remain. Confusion about its details is still possible. (If you doubt the possibility of confusion about picturing the mask symbol, tell the dream to three different people and ask them each to draw the golden mask; you will be surprised how differently the three drawings will turn out.)

Here are some immersion questions that people asked the dreamer about the golden mask in order to clarify its details:

- How thick was the mask?
- Were major facial features carved on it?
- Did it have other features such as hair, hairline, ears, eyebrows, dimples?

- Were any of these features sharp and clear?
- Did the mask show a distinct personality?
- Were there other openings than the nostrils and eyes?
- If the mask had no opening at the mouth, how could you hear the baby crying so clearly?
- Did the gold have a mouth shaped into it?
- Were the lips shaped open as if the mask was trying to speak?
- Did it look like anyone you know?
- How far down over the face did the mask go? To the neck? Past the neck?
- Was the mask heavy?
- Was it real gold?
- Was the baby able to lift its head with the mask on?
- Was there any sign of a seam in the metal?
- How tight was the mask to the head?
- Was the mask warm or cold?

Those who listened to her telling the dream spontaneously had answers to some of these questions because they pictured a golden mask in their imaginations as she told it. While you were reading the dream, the mask probably began to take shape for you, and it probably took on more detail as you envisioned answers to some of these questions. However, the mask now pictured in your imagination may not be the mask that the dreamer saw.

One way to ensure that you and the dreamer are seeing the same mask and working with the same image is to ask immersion questions like these, and adjust your image of the symbol as the dreamer answers each question.

Here's how the dreamer responded to the immersion questions:

*Those are all very good questions. Let me see. [Here the dreamer closed her eyes and re-created the dream scene with the aid of her imagination and memory. You could tell she had reentered the dream experience and was fully involved in it because, from time to time, her head turned as if she were looking to check some detail, and her fingers moved as if she were feeling to see how thick the mask was.]*

*The mask is about a quarter-inch thick. There are facial features, but only a minimum of them: a nose, ears, eyes, a mouth. Nothing distinctive like hair or hairline, cheekbones or dimples. Even the features that are there are not sharp or well-defined; they are only "suggested." For example, the mouth is just a slightly raised hint of lips, the ears just barely stand out from the rest of the head. There is no emotional expression on the mask. It looks more like an embryo than a child with personality and identity.*

*Everything about the mask is artistically smooth and stylized, like a piece of art. If you've ever seen a Henry Moore sculpture, you would know what I mean. Very beautiful and simple. Elegant.*

*There is no seam in the metal, and the mask reaches all the way down beneath the baby's chin, which means I cannot simply lift the mask off. The only openings in the mask, as I said, are the two nostril holes and the two eye slits.*

*I cannot explain how I am able to hear the baby's cries so loudly and clearly. Logically, I should never have been able to hear them in the first place. But, then, dreams aren't necessarily logical.*

*The mask's metal is warm. I suspect it's from the baby's body heat and crying. It also fits the head very tightly. The mask is solid gold and so heavy that the baby cannot hold its head up.*

The dreamer did not immediately know the answers to all the immersion questions asked of her, but she was able to re-create the dream scene in her imagination and observe the symbol in more detail there.

When you have a question about the details of a symbol, the answers to which you do not remember noticing in the dream, relax for a few moments, reenter the dream scene using your imagination and memory, and inspect the symbol so that you can see, feel, smell, hear, and touch it in all its details.

In relating what she learned about the symbol from doing symbol immersion, she replied:

*When I experienced the dream, I was caught up in my own response as mother to the baby in the golden mask. But while doing immersion on the mask symbol, I got a clearer*

sense of how confined and constricted the child was because of the mask. As I was doing the technique, I got in
touch with feelings of entrapment and constriction I have
known personally, and still know. In doing this technique,
I could already feel welling up inside me the energy to
begin removing my own mask and reclaiming the parts of
me that had been hidden and forgotten, neglected and not
nurtured. My awareness that the mask was crushing the
child's head and distorting its brain was frightening and
added to my sense of urgency.

To the questions people were asking, I heard myself
reply with metaphoric statements, such as, "The child is
not able to hold up its head because of the weight of the
mask," or "The gold mask was so shiny that I was able to
see a distorted reflection of myself in it." For me, not being
able to hold my head up meant that I sometimes lacked
respect for myself, didn't assert my rights, didn't take pride
in my accomplishments, devalued what I had to contribute. The distorted reflection hinted at a distorted self-
image, a personality built more on mostly negative reflections of what others expected me to be rather than on my
own internal identity.

In the dream, I ended up having two children, two
self-images, one loved and one unloved, one nurtured and
one not nurtured.

The fact that the mask prevented the baby from being
nourished struck me strongly. That baby had a right, just as
the "good little girl" baby in the next room had, to have
been receiving care and nourishment continuously since
birth. They had been born twins with an equal right to live
in the world. I could feel that right as my own right to live.

## TECHNIQUE 4: AMPLIFY THE SYMBOL

Once you have done Technique 3, Immerse Yourself in the
Symbol, you are ready to begin sorting out the issues and emotions
that the symbol evokes, and putting aside those that it doesn't.

The first step is to begin collecting a list of possible issues to
which the symbol might be pointing. There is a simple way to do
this, which is rather enjoyable. On a sheet of paper, list the many

different functions the symbol in general can serve in ordinary life. That is, how and for what do people use this symbol?

For example, if your symbol is a fire in a fireplace, ask yourself, "What are the different functions a fire in a fireplace serves?" Some functions might be: to cook something, to relax nearby, to create a romantic atmosphere, to warm the room, to have a special evening, to impress guests, to burn old papers, or to chase unwanted birds out of the chimney.

As each of these functions is mentioned, you will know whether or not the function is a "hit" or a "miss." A "hit" means that you, the dreamer, have a sense that this function applies to the symbol in your dream. In other words, it rings true for you. You will perceive some functions as hits and others as misses.

The objective of this technique is to clarify those issues of the dream that are related to the symbol, so that you know where to focus your dreamwork in order to begin releasing the energy and insight contained in the symbol.

In doing this technique, the mask dreamer worked with a few other people, all of whom suggested different functions of a mask. Dozens of functions were mentioned. As each one was suggested, the dreamer took a moment to check her inner response to it: Did it ring true for her or not? Some suggestions were definite hits, others were definite misses. A few were nearly hits, and in some of these cases the dreamer was able to modify the wording of the function slightly in order to turn it into a direct hit.

Here are some of the hits:

The function of a mask is:

- To conceal your true identity.
- To take on a different identity.
- To restrict your expression of feelings.
- To evoke certain responses from others.
- To provide a barrier between you and others.
- To constrict your expression. (This was changed by the dreamer to a direct hit as: To hide your expression and, therefore, your feelings.)
- To protect you from being hurt (as a catcher's mask in baseball).
- To imprison you.
- To change your appearance.

- To appear to be somebody else.
- To hide injury, scars or defects.
- To protect you during a time of healing (as bandages do).
- Something you can put on or take off at will.
- A work of art.
- To hide the truth. [This was a near hit; the dreamer was able to modify it so it became a direct hit: To hide one's true nature.]
- To wear to a party or masquerade. [Not a direct hit; but "To be acceptable in society" would be.]

Here are some of the misses:

The function of a mask is:

- To act in a play.
- To depict a person at a different point in time.
- To show signs of specialness, e.g., divinity.
- To liberate you to express non-ordinary emotions.
- To express the feminine.
- To make you look like other people (the uniform look).
- To allow you to pretend to be a child and play as children play.
- To hide your identity so you can steal (masked robber).
- To allow you to fool or play a joke on somebody.
- To create dis-ease in others (fear).
- Something you can buy in a store.
- Something you would mold over a dead person's face to preserve their memory (death mask).
- To honor someone.

The dreamer was asked to relate what she learned from doing this amplification technique:

*I'm aware the mask has protecting as well as constricting properties. In fact, hiding, making acceptable, and protecting are the predominant strategies and energies the mask provides me. The imprisoning and constricting as well as the barrier qualities feel more like what happened because of the mask than what was intended when the mask was first tried on. I am now beginning to feel attracted and impressed by some of the useful aspects of the*

*mask, whereas my original feeling toward it had been one*
*of repulsion.*

*I find myself drawn to the suggestion of the mask as*
*something that is meant to be put on or taken off at will.*
*However, the child in the dream does not have that ability.*
*The child is unable to take the mask off. The child needs a*
*nurturing mother's attention, and the mother needs to call*
*on a professional.*

*The "misses" help me see that the energy of the sym-*
*bol is not malevolent or frivolous.*

## TECHNIQUE 5: CARRY THE SYMBOL FORWARD IN TIME

Already from the first four symbol techniques, the dreamer has
gained many insights about the symbol and the functions it serves.
She has many avenues to pursue in doing growth work related to the
symbol.

However, she feels that the symbol's function in the dream is as
yet unresolved. It is unresolved on both ends of the dream. At the
beginning of the dream, she has no idea how the golden mask first
got put on the child. At the end of the dream, she does not know if
the mask will actually be removed and the child's life saved.

Technique 5 is designed to help answer the second question or,
more generally, "What happens to the symbol when you carry it into
the future?"

But how can you carry forward in time a dream that has ended?
Doesn't a dream end as soon as a person awakes? Not quite.

The events of a dream are not pieces of outer-life history, they
occur in the inner life of the dreamer. Access to this inner realm is
not restricted to the time of dreaming. In our day, people use a wide
variety of techniques to reenter that inner world, including meditation, contemplation, yoga, hypnotherapy, chanting, drama, sports,
drugs, or religious rituals.

It is not very difficult to enter the imaginal world and reconnect
with the images of a dream. Usually, all you have to do is relax a bit,
take a few deep breaths, begin retelling the dream, and let the dream
images come alive again in your imagination. Once you are back in
this state of active imagination, which we call a "waking dream"
state, you may reenter the dream and, in this technique, carry the
symbol forward in time (dream experience time).

If you were guiding the dreamer in this technique, you might say to her: "Let yourself relax and get back into the dream. Focus on the last scene in which the golden mask appeared. Remember, you were holding the baby in the golden mask, waiting for the goldsmith to come. When you have that scene vividly in your mind and imagination, keep watching the mask as you invite your imagination to move forward in time. Tell me aloud what is happening so that I can picture it too. Keep carrying the symbol forward in your imagination until it changes enough to give you some important information or to provide a sense of resolution."

In carrying the symbol forward, here's what the dreamer reported:

*I am reconnecting with the mask by reconnecting with the emotions I felt upon awakening the morning I had the dream: sadness, anxiety, frustration, and wanting. I am reexperiencing the last scene of the dream and letting my imagination carry the symbol forward in time.*

Here is her waking-dream report.

*DREAM REPORT (A WAKING DREAM EXPERIENCE)*

*I am waiting for the goldsmith in the baby's nursery. I am holding the child in the golden mask, supporting its head. The goldsmith comes in carrying a black bag. He examines the golden mask and asks if I have any special place I want the metal cut in order to remove it.*

*I say, "No. Just get it off the baby's head as quickly and safely as possible."*

*He opens his black bag revealing a variety of tools. He says he will probably cut directly behind the ears of the mask, across the top, from side to side, "so the mask will not be totally destroyed, for it is quite beautiful. The back of the mask will be separated from the front and the baby can then be freed."*

*I hold the child as he works, cutting through the gold mask. The baby is not as upset as I had feared it might be. Maybe it is fascinated by the new sounds and sensations. The process of removing the mask seems to absorb all of us.*

*Sometimes I get anxious that the child will be hurt, but the goldsmith seems to be working very confidently and skillfully.*

*Finally, the back of the mask has been completely cut through. He gently taps it in several places and the back part drops off into my hand. I gently maneuver the child free of the rest of the mask.*

*The goldsmith then asks me what I want to do with the gold mask. "The gold itself is very valuable," he says.*

*And I reply, "Good. It can be melted down and sold, and I'll use the money for nourishing other needy children."*

*The goldsmith says, "Yes, that can be done." He indicates that he himself would buy the gold from me, but he suggests that because the mask is also a work of art it would be much more valuable if preserved and sold to a museum. He says he can send some museum people to me.*

*The goldsmith asks me where I would like to put the mask in the meantime. I say, "On the mantel in the library." As we place the mask on the library mantel, I realize that it will eventually be displayed in a public place to be seen and enjoyed by many people, and the money from its purchase will be used for a home for needy or abandoned children. At this point, I feel the mask needs no more attention, and the baby does.*

First of all, the dreamer has been able to bring resolution to the role of the mask. (She still has to do symbol work with the child that had been in the golden mask. For this task, too, Technique 5, Carry the Symbol Forward in Time, would be a natural choice.)

She has also discovered new values of the mask, made a choice about what she will do with the mask and the proceeds from its sale, and established a working relationship with the professional goldsmith. Both the symbol of the mask and the symbol of the goldsmith have taken on a new richness. The energies that the mask symbol is ready to release into her life are beginning to clarify; they will soon be expressed in personality tasks and relationship tasks to be performed in her waking life (Techniques 9 through 16).

To describe what she learned from doing this technique, the dreamer replied:

*I realize I have already made contact with a professional who removes masks. Several weeks before the dream, I had contracted for a personal therapy process which was to begin when I returned from the month-long colloquium. The therapist was a woman, well-known for her professional skill and her expertise with many therapeutic techniques (like the tools of the goldsmith).*

*In the dream, I couldn't remove the mask all by myself. (Doing things all by myself would have been my usual mode and one that would become an issue in therapy—the need to develop the ability to ask for help.)*

*Reaching out to a professional was to be lived out in both inner and outer life: I worked with a professional therapist in the outer world, while at the same time I developed internally a "professional within" through the process of internalization. In both my inner and outer worlds, I was also developing myself and my identity as a "professional," as I finished my Ph.D. in clinical psychology. Not surprisingly, I had specialized in child psychology and child development.*

*I also realized that the male professional (goldsmith) spoke to my need to develop a relationship to my masculine side. This energy was also suggested in the dream when I made an effort to use my logical, analytical, decisive qualities.*

## TECHNIQUE 6: CARRY THE SYMBOL BACKWARD IN TIME

This technique is rather unusual, and many people ask, "Why carry the symbol back in time?" The simple reason is that the dreamer and her partners wondered where the golden mask had come from. "How did it get there in the first place?"

This is a very important question, because the symbol techniques completed so far indicate the usefulness of the mask as a defense mechanism, and are pointing to issues of identity and childhood. It would be important to know some of the sources of these issues. The origins of the golden mask are very likely to provide important clues. Carrying the symbol backward in time is good for uncovering such sources.

The technique involves the dreamer entering the waking dream state, as in the previous technique, except that the instructions this time request the dreamer to observe the symbol and let her imagination take her back in time to reveal the origins or history of the golden mask.

Here's what the dreamer reported:

*To do this technique, I am getting centered. I focus briefly on the symbol, and then I let my mind go quiet, like a blank screen where new images can appear. In whatever way it happens, I am open to seeing the symbol in its origins or in an earlier period. I experience this as a waking dream.*

*DREAM REPORT (A WAKING DREAM EXPERIENCE)*

*I see a dark room with a crib in it. It is the baby's nursery. The baby is asleep in the crib. Slowly, the door opens and a woman holding a candle walks into the room, almost like someone walking in her sleep. Holding the candle high, she leans over the baby's crib as if to check on the child. As the candle flickers, she turns to look at the flame, and the gold scarf she is wearing on her head slips off and falls over the sleeping infant's head. She does not notice the scarf has fallen, but seems absorbed in the candle flame. Although she is physically in the room, she is not really present, for she seems unaware of the infant, its needs, and its reality. She leaves the room without ever having looked at the infant, and it sleeps on with the gold scarf over its head. The child moves in its sleep and, in time, the scarf becomes tightly wound about the baby's head, encasing the head in its goldness. The mother never returns, and eventually the golden head covering hardens into the golden mask.*

When asked how this technique had helped her understand herself in any way, the dreamer replied:

*The mother of the child is unconscious of the child and its endangerment. She is really not present to the child, its needs, and its reality. That is probably a very accurate state-*

ment about my childhood and my mother's relationship to me. She was physically present but never involved, never caretaking, never emotionally connected, mostly unaware of me. It is interesting that the mask evolved from a golden head covering because the only positive qualities of my mother I can name are that she was physically beautiful in an exotic, Spanish-looking sort of way (so the gold head covering fits that). Also, she was known to have been intellectually brilliant in high school and had gone on to college, reflecting valuable qualities having to do with the head. My identity has always had to do with being pretty and wondering about being smart enough, so my own mask has had to do with being beautiful and having valuable "head" qualities. I guess I had bonded with the only part of her available to me.

This experience brings me some sense of relief, an awareness that it was not my fault that my mother didn't care for me. It wasn't that I was unlovable; it was just that my mother didn't see me or connect with me. She was not conscious of me or, for that matter, able to relate to people in general. She was indeed like a sleepwalker.

## TECHNIQUE 7: ASSOCIATE TO THE SYMBOL

The symbol technique that you may be most familiar with is symbol association, a simple process of linking images spontaneously. It involves repeatedly answering the question "What does that remind you of?" or "What association do you make to that image or word?"

Symbol association is usually led by a dream partner or a counselor, who agrees to keep asking you the question: "And what does THAT remind you of?" until you experience a hit, an insight or a connection that is meaningful to you. The technique usually works rather quickly, sometimes in even less than a minute. When it works, it often helps clarify key issues related to the symbols that are active in your life today and, as in the case with the golden mask, reveals some of the roots of those issues.

As a dreamwork partner, it is important that you stop the process when the dreamer has a hit. When a hit occurs, assume that it is the piece of information they have been digging for. Usually you can recognize a hit in the dreamer's facial expression, or you can simply ask the dreamer to tell you when a hit has occurred. If the process seems to reach a dead end, you can always go back and start the process afresh.

If the dreamer is responding abstractly to your questions, encourage her to answer by naming concrete pictures or images. For example, if she replies, "It reminds me of childhood," (which is too vague a response), ask her, "What scene in childhood does it remind you of?" Keep requesting images. The power of the symbol is locked in its image, not in an abstract idea or concept.

Here's the way the association technique went for the dreamer when it began with the golden mask:

Partner:   *What does the golden mask in your dream remind you of?*
Dreamer:  *A Henry Moore sculpture.*
Partner:   *And what does a Henry Moore sculpture remind you of?*
Dreamer:  *A beautiful piece of sculpture that I have in my garden, which I bought because it reminded me of a Henry Moore sculpture.*
Partner:   *And what does that piece of sculpture in your garden remind you of?*
Dreamer:  *Its title, which is "Supplication."*
Partner:   *And what does the title "Supplication" remind you of?*
Dreamer:  *The sculpture is of a begging child, so it reminds me of a supplicating, begging child.*
Partner:   *And what does a begging child remind you of?*
Dreamer:  *A deprived child.*
Partner:   *And what does a deprived child remind you of?*
Dreamer:  *Myself as a deprived child, begging for love and attention, begging not to be hurt.*

At this point, it was clear that a "hit" had occurred, because with this last response the dreamer displayed a strong shift in emotion.

If as a dreamer's partner you are not certain whether a hit has occurred, simply ask the dreamer.

The work of the various symbol techniques on the golden mask are beginning to converge on the key issues in the dreamer's life and their sources.

When asked what she learned from this technique, the dreamer replied:

> *It underlines the basic information about my wearing a mask as a way to get the love and acceptance as well as the protection and attention I needed. It places the origins of the mask in the early childhood dynamics between my mother and myself. I knew the facts of the deprivation and abuse in my childhood but not their effects. The dream hinted at some of the ways I had adapted or protected myself. Now I understand some of what must be healed before the mask can be removed.*
>
> *I also realize that the mask, like the sculpture in my garden, can be beautiful and valuable, a real delight to see—in the right setting. I realize that having a mask to wear can be valuable and helpful to me in the right circumstances, in an appropriate placement, so to speak. As a therapist, for instance, being pretty and sweet helps in appearing nonthreatening to many of the children I work with and, therefore, in developing a therapeutic relationship with them.*

## TECHNIQUE 8: NAME SOME ENERGIES RELATED TO THE SYMBOL

Up to now, all the symbol techniques were designed primarily to reveal issues, problems, and sources of problems. What about the energies, insights, and information that will help deal with those issues and resolve some of those problems? Are those resources reflected in the symbol as well? Yes.

With this technique, you begin examining the symbol in terms of the energies it symbolizes, energies which are available to you for working on your growth issues.

If your deep inner self presents you with a dream that focuses your attention on a certain issue, your deep inner self is also ready to help you work on that issue for your own growth and wholeness. If you were *not* ready to deal with the issue at certain levels, your inner self would not have given you the dream, nor would your conscious mind likely "see" the issues and feel them as "hits."

This technique is based on the spiritual growth principle: *If a dream (or symbol) naturally brings an issue or problem to the level of conscious awareness, it indicates you have the energies, strength, insight, ability, etc. to begin dealing with that issue or problem.*

To do this technique, the dreamer is first asked to review the results of earlier techniques and gather a list of the major issues that need to be addressed.

Next, beneath each issue, the dreamer is asked to draw up a sublist of the energies, skills, and qualities she thinks she will need in order to begin dealing successfully with those issues. The energies, skills, and qualities she will put on these lists are some of the ones most likely being released by the dream symbol.

When the dreamer was asked to make a list of the key issues in her life and growth, revealed by the symbol work on the golden mask, she wrote:

1. *Personal identity (finding out who I really am)*
2. *Relationship to my mother*
3. *Acknowledging childhood hurts and abuse*
4. *Lack of assertiveness (e.g., not able to express my rights because I focus on being good, sweet, pretty, gentle, etc.)*
5. *Integration of masculine and feminine energies in me (only feminine is strong now)*
6. *Not able to express my needs and wants (It isn't "nice" to ask.)*
7. *Not able to let others help me (I have wanted to be strong, to hide weaknesses, imperfections, etc.)*
8. *Learning how to use the "mask" healthily and appropriately*

Getting a start from a list of typical energies for growth released by symbols, found in Part 3 of this book, she created sublists of energies and skills beneath each of her eight key issues. Here's how her sublists looked:

1. PERSONAL IDENTITY
accepting the weak & ugly
patience
wholeness & balance
child energy
ability to hide
to transform myself
to reveal myself

2. RELATIONSHIP WITH
   MOTHER
ability to protect myself
self-esteem
unconditional love
forgiveness
healing
acceptance
receiving

3. CHILDHOOD HURTS
healing
nurturing energy
caretaking energy
to liberate and set free
specialness & attention
playfulness & creativity

4. LACK OF ASSERTIVENESS
to be frightening (threatening
   or confronting)
anger
ability to be strong and hard
courage
self-affirmation
make myself heard
determination

5. INTEGRATE MASCULINE
action-taking
integration
logical thinking
fortitude (strength)
decisiveness & discrimination
courage

6. EXPRESS WANTS
wanting attention
wanting nourishment
wanting to be held, loved,
   cared for, played with, etc.
wanting to own & value
   what is mine

7. LETTING OTHERS HELP
to feel given-to, or nurtured
to be defended & comforted
to be receptive
to feel valued
to accept my preciousness
to cry out for help (request)

8. HEALTHY USES OF MASK
to bring beauty & delight into
   the world
to attract attention and caring
to express my beauty and value
to express my brightness
to remind me of freedom

In relating what she had learned from this exercise, she said:

*I can see on the list many energies that I want to express, to
have access to, and use. I can begin to think of instances in*

the past where I have needed those energies, and places in the present where I might practice calling on them. I also get a sense of the complexity of my personality, what my wholeness might begin to look like. I can feel myself wanting these energies, all of them, and I can sense being especially attracted to certain ones.

My first thought is to choose one from each category to begin focusing on. For instance, in #1, accepting the weak and ugly parts of myself, such as finding and exploring shadow energies. In #2, the ability to protect myself by standing up for my rights and confronting others.

*Chapter 3*

# SYMBOL WORK—ACTION TECHNIQUES

## SYMBOL WORK TECHNIQUES THAT LEAD TO ACTION

Working with all these insights about issues and lists of available energies can get a bit overwhelming. With such an overflow of information, the dreamer may not know where to begin. What does it all mean? What does all this have to do with spiritual growth and wholeness? Now that the dreamer is conscious of these insights and energies, what's the next step? How can the dreamer make them work effectively for herself?

In the context of personal growth, the word consciousness has two levels: the first is the level of *awareness* (the level to which the first eight symbol techniques have brought the dreamer); the second is the level of *appropriate action,* (the level upon which the next eight symbol techniques focus).

*Consciousness is defined as awareness plus appropriate action.* Awareness without action is still not consciousness. To be conscious means you have taken the insights and energies revealed and released by the symbol and turned them into appropriate action in your daily life.

The following eight symbol techniques are designed to help you begin to put into action the energies and insights you gained from the first eight symbol techniques. The first of these action techniques is to have a dialogue with the symbol.

## TECHNIQUE 9: DIALOGUE WITH THE SYMBOL

Dialogue is a very powerful technique that is carried out in a waking dream state. During this waking dream, you befriend the symbol and build an in-depth relationship with it. If the symbol is impersonal, as is the golden mask, treat it as if it were a person who could talk to you. Give the symbol a name such as "Golden Mask," and address it by that name.

Dialogue is an ideal way to deal with unanswered questions you may have about the symbol. You may also ask the symbol for wisdom to clarify and use wisely the energies revealed by it. Specifically, you may ask where to use your new-found energies in your daily life and relationships.

Usually, before a dialogue, you prepare a few questions to address to the symbol. Most dreamers, as soon as they reflect for a minute, can jot down half-a-dozen questions they would like to ask the symbol. These questions may be specific ("Mask, at what age was the child when you were put on her?") or general ("Mask, what is your meaning in my life?")

The dialogue technique is most often done by recording your inner conversation with the symbol as it comes to you. We recommend writing it out. Of course, you may simply do the dialogue "in your head," but then you have no record of the details of it.

Some people are afraid that, as soon as they begin writing, the waking dream will vanish and the flow of communication will stop. Don't worry, you can easily stay in the waking dream state and write at the same time.

To begin, relax and let the symbol come alive in your mind and imagination. See yourself present to the symbol as to a friend with whom you are about to have a conversation.

Open the dialogue by writing down your first question, and picture yourself asking the question to the symbol. Then, write down whatever response seems to come into your mind.

Some people feel that the responses come from themselves, not the symbol. Of course, the response comes from within you; you are having a dialogue with your deep inner self or your soul, and the symbol merely provides a vehicle for the interaction.

Even though it feels forced at first, continue writing out the dialogue. After a few exchanges, it becomes easier, and you will begin to notice that there are really two "voices" dialoguing.

Remember, you are now at the stage where you want to put the insights of the dream into action. So, as part of the dialogue, ask the symbol how you can specifically apply its wisdom and energies.

Some people generate pages of dialogue, others only a few lines. Write until the dialogue naturally ends or has produced some sense of resolution.

Here is a dialogue that the dreamer had with the golden mask:

Dreamer: *Mask, what am I to learn from you?*

Mask: *Look at me, see my qualities. Recognize what I have brought you and what I have cost you.*

Dreamer: *That sounds scary, but I do want to learn. I do want to be more whole.*

Mask: *Your wanting is good energy to start with. Develop it.*

Dreamer: *I want to know what you have brought me.*

Mask: *I want you to work to discover this for yourself, but I will get you started. I have brought you survival in childhood, popularity in high school, and security in your marriage. I have kept you living in your own world, free from the awareness of the dangers and realities of the larger world. I have kept you childlike and known as pretty, sweet, charming, desirable, and non-threatening.*

Dreamer: *Will I have to lose all those qualities if I take the mask off?*

Mask: *You will not necessarily lose them, but you will have to develop some of the opposite qualities they represent as well, in order to bring balance into your life.*

Dreamer: *What has been the cost of you?*

Mask: *Again, I would like you to reflect on this for yourself, but I will get you started. You have named some of these costs yourself in the "Amplification." You are imprisoned, your true self is hidden, your self-image and thinking is being distorted, you can barely hear or see the real world, you live a restricted life, and your true self is starving to death, crying out for attention and nourishment.*

Dreamer: *I can see that. I cannot truly "hold up my head" with self-esteem if I am known and valued only as a mask.*

Mask: *Yes, that is the idea. Continue reflecting and applying those insights to your life.*

Dreamer: *Thank you, Mask.*

When asked what she learned about practical applications to her life from this technique, this was her reply:

*The naming of the energy of "wanting" as a good place to start is profound. Usually, I avoid wanting and making choices. I realize my personality is not based on my want-ing, but on trying to figure out what I should want or what others would have me want. I am not grounded in my own life through wants that express me.*

*It is useful to acknowledge what the mask has brought me and to affirm its value. I can see why it is precious to me. I realize I don't want to lose some of its qualities and I will have to figure out what the opposite qualities would be that I also need to develop for balance. I can see that the list of energies [Technique 8] probably already contains them in some form.*

*I acknowledge how high the cost of wearing the mask has been, and I need to realize that I cannot go on paying that price and live. I must choose life. It is a spiritual choice, for the life of my soul as well as my psyche is at stake.*

## TECHNIQUE 10: CREATE EXPRESSIVE ARTWORK BASED ON THE SYMBOL

One of the most concrete ways to bring the energy of the symbol into your life is to capture the symbol in some expressive physical form. The purpose of this technique is to give the symbol physical presence in your life. The simplest way is to draw the symbol on a piece of paper.

Others have represented their symbol in sculpture using wood, clay, metal, or paper. Still others have written poems or songs about their symbol. Some have created a dance about their symbol and danced it. Others have turned their dream into a story, skit, mime, fairy tale, or drama. Many have created a mandala, collage, or a painting to express it. Often there are new insights in this process. Find some way to record or acknowledge them.

It doesn't matter that you feel unqualified to draw or paint or sing or dance, since this is not a test of your artistic abilities. The intent of the technique is to release the energy of the symbol. Its purpose is to help you produce something visible, something you can tack on your wall, tape on your refrigerator, lay on your dresser, hang from the ceiling, or even wear. Every time you look at it or hear it or dance it or sing it, you are reminded of an energy for your wholeness that is alive and kicking inside you. Cherish your symbolic artwork and let it remind you to call upon the symbol's energies for your self-transformation.

To get you oriented, begin by making a list of the different forms you could use to express the symbol. For example, how many different ways could you recommend to the golden-mask dreamer to embody her mask in an art form?

Ways that spontaneously come to mind include: drawing the mask, sculpting it, writing a poem about it, buying a mask and painting it as the golden mask, making a collage of people wearing masks. When the dreamer carried the mask symbol forward in time, she placed the mask on the mantel in her library. Perhaps in waking life she might do the same with her drawing or sculpture.

Interestingly, no one in the group who listened to her dream at the Florida colloquium suggested to the dreamer that she embody her golden mask in some expressive art form. Or, if they did, she did not follow through on their suggestion. However, some time later, very naturally, the opportunity to complete this technique appeared when she took part in a mask-making workshop.

MASK-MAKING EXPERIENCE

*Nine months after the original mask dream, I attended a week-long conference on therapeutic techniques. During the conference, I participated in a mask-making experience. A mask of wet plaster was made on my face by a partner using strips of gauze dipped in liquid plaster. As directed by the workshop leader, my partner left a slight opening for each nostril and for each eye, but I silently signaled a special request that the mouth on my mask was to be closed over.*

*In this process, my face is greased ahead of time, so when the mask is finished I remove it by leaning forward and letting it fall off my face. When I sat up, leaned forward, and let the mask fall off my face into my own hands, I thought, "That is the way to remove a mask, let it fall into your own hands."*

*Each one's mask was to be painted and decorated after it dried. Everyone noted that my painted mask was exceptionally beautiful.*

*After I returned home, I meditated on the mask and tried to dialogue with it. I sensed it could not speak with its closed mouth, so I took a razor blade and opened the lips just slightly so it could at least whisper to me.*

In describing what she discovered about herself from creating a plaster mask, the dreamer replied:

*I realized that the qualities of the mask didn't have to be lost. As long as they were in my own hands, the mask quali- ties could be used, taken off, and put back on at will. I was no longer imprisoned by the mask but neither had it lost its usefulness. I could still be "beautiful" when I wanted to.*

*I realized that not speaking, not having an opinion, not requesting, not confronting, not defending myself verbally were very much a part of the way I stayed "sweet and non- threatening." I wanted to change that, at least so I could know my own thoughts, opinions, wants, and feelings.*

*I placed the mask in my library, on the top bookshelf where I saw it whenever I sat at my desk. Presently it is outside my bedroom closet where I can see it daily as I go to dress (selecting a persona).*

## TECHNIQUE 11: MEDITATE ON THE SYMBOL

The dreamer instinctively chose to meditate using her mask as a focal point. In light of her spiritual growth, she realized a need to integrate the symbol into her conscious, daily life. To do this she used the plaster mask to symbolize the golden mask in her dream, which had for so long been hidden from her consciousness. When- ever she wanted, she could hold the plaster mask in her hands and look at it, and be reminded of the insights and energies the dream symbol had provided.

During meditation, an activity usually dedicated to personal transformation, you have the opportunity to cherish a dream symbol as a reminder of your call to wholeness and holiness. Meditation provides a time to rest quietly in the presence of your symbol.

It is not necessary to have made a sculpture or drawing inspired by your symbol in order to meditate upon it. You may meditate holding an image of the symbol in your imagination, or you may repeat the name of your symbol and the energy you want, using a kind of repetitive chant or mantra. Set aside at least ten minutes for a meditative time, and be sure to write your reflections on paper when your meditation is over.

The dreamer used the plaster mask she had made in the workshop as a focus for her meditation on the dream symbol, the golden mask. Here are her reflections:

*The mask is beautiful. I need to appreciate its beauty. I realize, however, that no work of art can be as beautiful as the human baby in the other nursery, so no mask can be as beautiful as a truly human person. I am encouraged to seek my true humanness.*

*When the mask is first removed, I sense the baby will look ugly since, for a long time, its skin has not had contact with air and light. It will take a while for the baby's skin to adjust and heal, and I must have patience and love and believe in what the baby will become.*

*To be without my mask may be painful. To see the larger world and the mother may be unfamiliar and frightening. Certainly, to truly see the world in its present condition of nuclear threat, prejudice, hunger, disease, pollution, is frightening. To see my childhood and my relationship to my mother as it truly was is painful. To let many feelings, long hidden from myself as well as the outer world, come into consciousness is frightening. I had painted golden tears on the plaster mask and I sensed the sadness I have avoided feeling and expressing.*

*I can begin to clarify the tasks awaiting me and set some goals:*

1. *In the dream, the features on the mask are almost ambiguous, undifferentiated. I need to know my features, see my characteristics more clearly, and develop an identity, a sense of self and self-esteem. I also need to know how others truly see me.*
2. *In the dream, I am aware that the masked baby feels anger, aggressiveness, wanting, hunger, pain, deprivation, and sadness. I must acknowledge, explore, and own these feelings in myself and allow for their expression in my personality and the world.*

3. *I need to develop within me the masculine energies and integrate them with my feminine energies. For example, I could begin by listing these energies and seeing how I do or do not use them in my life presently.*
4. *In the dream, I connect with a masculine figure (the goldsmith) in order to remove the mask. I will need to connect with my masculine energies, i.e., thinking, focusing, analyzing, asserting, making an impact on the world, becoming an authority and a dragon-slaying hero, etc., in order to cut through the mask. I will need discrimination and logic to identify and develop the various energies, courage to risk and face change, patience for them to begin to work, and trust in the process.*

## TECHNIQUE 12: RESEARCH THE SYMBOL

Now that you have a firm grasp of your symbol, its meanings, insights, and the energies it can release in you, you may turn to others for confirmation of your symbol work, or for an expansion of it.

What, for example, are some of the cultural, historical, biblical, and archetypal roots of your symbol? Is your symbol found in nursery rhymes, fairy tales, classical myths, short stories, great novels, famous movies, popular television shows, plays, biblical episodes, songs, pieces of music, sacred writings, psychological theories, primitive practices, cliches, figures of speech?

How have others interpreted your symbol and used it? Did Freud mention it? Did Jung use it? What do the symbol books say about it? How about other writers who discuss archetypal material?

Have you encountered the same or similar symbols in previous dreams or in your waking life? If you went back and researched your own personal dream journal, what would it tell you about your symbol? Has it ever occurred before? Was it ever as powerful as this? Was this symbol ever something used by your own family, e.g., in a family anecdote handed down from generation to generation?

In doing this technique, when you establish a connection, say, between your symbol and a passage in the Bible, ask yourself: "How does this connection speak to me about my current way of being, acting, choosing, or relating? What energies might this connection be releasing in me and how could I put them to use in my life today?"

Many of the alternatives in this technique had little or no appeal to the dreamer. She was not interested in exploring the literature that contained stories about masks. Someone mentioned to her the classic French novel by Alexandre Dumas (1802–1870), *The Man in the Iron Mask,* but she did not know of the novel and had never seen the film.

"The golden mask reminds me of no songs, no family stories, nothing in the Bible," she said. "In art museums, I recall seeing African masks that were wooden and dark, but they don't remind me of the golden mask. As I said before, the mask in my dream reminds me of a Henry Moore sculpture and the sculpture in my garden, not of Greek masks used in ancient drama. I do know that Halloween was always my favorite holiday. I could ask for 'treats' and even do naughty 'tricks' from the safety of a disguise."

She supposed the mask symbol had not occurred before in her dreams, though until the mask dream, she was not accustomed to keeping a dream journal and so had no way to verify her supposition.

As a student of clinical psychology and a reader of mythology, she knew Carl Jung had written about masks and their psychological function. One of her chosen tasks was to research Jung's writings on the *persona,* the Greek word for mask. Jung believed the *persona* was a major archetype in the constellation of archetypes that orbited within the collective unconscious universe. Its function was to energize a person's social or public faces.

In *An Introduction to Jung's Psychology* by Frieda Fordham, she found the following:

> The process of civilizing the human being leads to a compromise between himself and society as to what he should appear to be, and to the formation of the mask behind which most people live. Jung calls this mask the *persona,* the name given to the masks once worn by the actors of antiquity to signify the role they played. But it is not only actors who fill a role, a man who takes up a business or a profession, a woman who marries or chooses a career, all adopt to some extent the characteristics expected of them in their chosen position; it is necessary to do so in order to succeed. A businessman will try to appear (and even to be)

forceful and energetic, a professional man intelligent, a civil servant correct; a professional woman nowadays needs not only to appear intelligent but also well dressed, and a wife is required to be a hostess, a mother, a partner, or whatever her husband's position demands.

Society expects, and indeed must expect, every individual to play the part assigned to him as perfectly as possible, so that a man who is a parson . . . must at all times . . . play the role of parson in a flawless manner. Society demands this as a kind of surety: each must stand at his post, here a cobbler, there a poet. No man is expected to be both . . . that would be "odd." Such a man would be "different" from other people, not quite reliable. In the academic world he would be a dilettante, in politics an "unpredictable" quantity, in religion a free-thinker—in short, he would always be suspected of unreliability and incompetence, because society is persuaded that only the cobbler who is not a poet can supply workmanlike shoes. (C.G. Jung, *Two Essays on Analytical Psychology,* par. 305)

From early childhood, the dreamer realized what society expected of her and tried to live up to its expectations.

*I realized I had been wearing the "good girl" mask since childhood, hiding hurt feelings, anger, sadness, and even physical pain. When I was abused as a child, I didn't cry for myself, but when I returned to my room, I would cry for the child with her ugly red welts and bruises whom I saw reflected in the mirror. Later, as a married woman, the good girl mask evolved into the "perfect wife" mask. As I perceived it, the perfect wife had all the good girl qualities plus being pretty, sweet, agreeable, soft-spoken, gentle, hard-working, affectionate, and intelligent (but only at those times when my husband considered a show of my intelligence appropriate). As a mother, I was also determined to star in the "perfect mother" role.*

*I liked the admiration I received for doing well in my roles, the security of being liked. But I also felt restless and vaguely fearful. In fact, I had a recurring nightmare from*

*which I always awoke crying, lying on a thoroughly soaked
pillow.*

*In the dream, my husband wanted something more
from me, and I couldn't figure out what that something
was. The thought that he might leave me before I discovered what it was he desired of me was terrifying. If he
would just wait, I thought, I would surely find it and give it
to him. In the dream, I would be crying as I pleaded with
him to wait just a little longer.*

*What had I not given him?*

*I think I had somehow hidden away my true self, my
soul, in such a way that neither my mother nor my husband
or family could take it away. I wasn't yet in touch with it, so
even I couldn't give it away to my husband.*

*It was the person behind the mask that was the true
self, the whole person, but I didn't know that then. I
thought the mask was me.*

Many people identify with their masks, instead of realizing their
masks are only a part of who they truly are. Once the dreamer could
discover the creator of the golden mask behind the mask and take
responsibility for choosing what masks she wanted to wear and
when she wanted to wear them, she would have in her own hands
the power to make and apply the masks she wore. She realized that
without masks, she might not appear with an agreeable face, but she
might be much more human and whole and able to take care of
herself in the real world.

## TECHNIQUE 13: ASK KEY QUESTIONS ABOUT THE SYMBOL

One of the most elusive aspects of dreamwork is how to keep
the symbol's energies alive after the dream is over. Certain symbol
techniques, such as dialoguing with the symbol, creating expressive
artwork based on the symbol, and meditating on the symbol, can
help keep the energies alive. The Key Questions technique also
works well for focusing energies.

The dreamer who is using dreamwork as a practice for holistic
growth has the opportunity to carry the dream energy into daily life.
In order to relate to the symbol with consciousness, insights must

become data upon which actions are performed and choices are made.

The Key Questions technique responds to the question the dreamer asks: "How else can I explore the symbol and put its energies into action right now?"

The best key questions are those created by the dreamer and the partners who know the dreamer and her dreams. Some general key questions are provided below, but they are to be used simply as starting questions to prime the pump of your own mind. You and your dream partners best know how you can put the energies of the symbol into action right now.

Here are a few sample key questions. A more complete list may be found in Part III of this book under Symbol Technique 13.

### Some Key Symbol Questions

- In the dream, why am I acting toward the symbol the way I'm acting?
- How are other dream figures relating to the symbol?
- Would I like to be relating to the symbol in a different way?
- Why might I need this symbol and its energies now?
- Does this symbol evoke a question about how I live my life?
- How is this symbol a gift to me now?

Not all generic key questions will apply to all symbols. That is why it's best to create your own key questions, ones that will force you to relate to the symbol in ways that affect the ways you act, choose, relate, and respond.

The dreamer of the mask dream answered some of the general key questions listed above, but found it even more focusing to invent, with the help of dreamwork partners, questions of her own. Here are some of those questions followed by her responses to them:

- In the dream, why am I acting toward the golden mask the way I am acting? And would I like to be relating to the mask in a different way; for example, the way the goldsmith does?
  *I am acting with shock, anxiety, frustration, and impatience toward the mask. I am anxious to face the child within and nourish it. I could use some of the goldsmith's thoughtful approach and*

*his confidence that the mask can be removed safely. In my waking dream he is gentle with me, the baby, and the mask. He is sensitive, caring, reassuring, and methodical in removing the mask. He sees the removal of the mask as a task to be done well rather than as a fearful situation.*

■ How might I need the energies released by the golden mask in decisions I need to make this week?
*It will help me remember that I want to be more assertive. I can ask questions, for instance, of the garage mechanic, instead of being "nice" by remaining silent.*

■ Where in my life am I wearing a mask today? Do I want to wear a mask there? Is there anywhere in my life where a mask is helpful?
*I frequently use the old, familiar mask-energy of hiding, but I would like to use some new energies. For instance: I often say "thank you" to someone when I really feel taken advantage of by them. I hide my negative feelings. I say "That's okay" when someone pushes in front of me in line and then, as an afterthought, asks if I mind. I would like to assert my rights—to tell them not only that I mind, but that they cannot do it.*

■ If there was one mask in my life that I'd want to get rid of right now, what would that be? How would I be different if I got rid of that mask?
*I'd like to get rid of the mask of appearing agreeable whenever anything is asked of me. I would like the energy to recognize what choices I have and discern what in my heart I want to choose, and to choose it.*

■ Where would be the easiest place or situation for me to start to remove that mask? Could I do it all at once, or would I have to do it in stages? What would be the first stage?
*Probably with my children: to be more conscious of my needs, and to realize that a choice for me is not necessarily being selfish and a bad mother. I could ask my children for help with the household tasks more often.*

After answering these key symbol questions about the mask, the dreamer had this to say about what she learned about her way of being, acting, choosing, and relating:

> *I realized that when someone makes a request of me I feel as though I "should" do it if I possibly can. Also, if I don't agree to do it, for whatever reason, and the person is disappointed, I feel bad. I remember once hearing a workshop leader say, "A choice for me is not necessarily a choice against you." Sometimes I would like to be able to say something like that to people who make requests of me. I need to examine many of the "should" feelings in my life.*
>
> *I thought about the women in my life whom I found most interesting, the ones I admired, and I asked myself if they tended to be assertive or agreeable. When I thought about it, I found they were a balance of both. While they were mostly agreeable, they were able to say No, to make requests, and assert their rights. I realized these women would be good models for me, so I chose to spend more time with them, develop their friendship, and learn from them.*
>
> *The first stage in my program would involve catching the "should" feelings as soon as they surfaced and not wearing the mask of agreeableness at all times. I realized this might be a slow and not altogether painless process.*

## TECHNIQUE 14: DO PERSONALITY TASKS

This technique and the one following are very practical techniques. They ask the dreamer to set herself tasks based on the symbol work, and to carry out those tasks. The heart of both techniques is to design tasks that are:

- finite
- time-limited
- measurable
- do-able by the dreamer
- related to the symbol's energies

Tasks that have these five qualities are most likely to succeed. In the process of self-transformation and spiritual growth, success is very important. Success builds on success. A series of small successes breeds a sense of self-confidence and larger success. Failure is a turn-off. When, as a dreamer or dream partner, you are designing or suggesting tasks for the dreamer to do to keep the energies of the dream alive and to incarnate those energies into everyday life, make sure those tasks possess all five of those qualities.

If a task is *not finite* ("List all the times in your life when you have acted from behind a mask"), you can never succeed in completing it.

If a task is *not time-limited* ("Don't ever let yourself hide your true feelings again"), you will never know when the task is over. If a task has no time boundaries, it must go on forever, it quickly becomes a burden and, as soon as you forget to do it, it generates a sense of guilt and failure.

If a task is *not measurable* ("Be assertive with your spouse"), you will never be able to know if you have completed it or done enough.

If the task is *not do-able by the dreamer* ("Read Jung's article on *persona* in the original German"), it generates immediate frustration and no hope of success.

If the task is *not based on the symbol's energy* ("Buy Christmas presents for your daughters by September 1st"), you cannot be sure the energy to carry out the task is available.

Each of those sample tasks suggested in parentheses, doomed to produce failure as stated, can be easily revised to possess the five qualities of a successful task:

An infinite task such as "List all the times in your life when you have acted from behind a mask" can easily be made *finite:* "List ten times in your life when you have acted from behind a mask."

A task without any time boundaries such as "Don't ever let yourself hide your true feelings again" can be given *some limits and deadlines:* "On each day for the next week, choose one hour during your workday when you will be true to yourself and for that hour tell people, when they ask you for something, what you really feel."

The non-measurable task "Be assertive with your spouse" can become the *easily-measurable:* "Be assertive with your spouse once each day for the next two weeks."

Because the dreamer cannot read German and wouldn't know where to look for Jung's writings in German, the suggested undoable task "Read Jung's article on *persona* in the original German" can become the *do-able* task: "Read one article on *persona* written by Jung or by someone else."

"Buy Christmas presents for your daughters before September 1st" can be made appropriate by *focusing the task on the symbol's energy:* "Let at least one of the Christmas presents you buy for your daughters this year reflect your wish for them to become assertive young women."

The tasks in this technique are to be aimed at the dreamer's *inner life and personality.* The tasks in the following technique are to be aimed at the dreamer's *outer life and relationships.* When a task is suggested, do not quibble over whether it is a personality task or a relationship task; just make sure it has the five qualities that lead to success.

Here are some of the personality tasks that were suggested to the dreamer to bring the mask symbol's energies into her inner life:

## Suggested Personality Tasks

- List three parts of your personality that have been hidden and forgotten and that you would like to reclaim.
- List two parts of your personality that still go without nourishment.
- List five situations where you tend to wear a mask.
- List five of your rights as a woman that you give up when you wear the "good girl" mask.
- List three situations where wearing a mask (persona) may be appropriate.
- List three books that might be useful to read to develop assertiveness.
- Read one of the books on your list within three months.
- List three novels and three films in which the heroine is a strong female role model.
- Read one of these books (or see one of these films) during the next three months.
- List the names of ten women who have at least one quality you would like to develop based on the mask dream. After each woman's name, list the quality or qualities you admire in her and want to emulate.

■ List three areas in your life where you could really use some outside help, if only you would ask for it.

■ List as many as five so-called masculine qualities that you would like to possess.

■ List three areas in your personal growth where you need to be patient.

■ List five times during the past year or so when you felt anger and wanted to express it, but didn't because you wanted to maintain your "sweet" image.

The dreamer did not do every one of these personality tasks, and she actually developed and carried out some others not on this list. Because all of the suggested tasks were finite, time-limited, measurable, do-able, and related to the symbol's energies, she experienced much success in the tasks she did and managed to keep the symbol energy alive in her life.

One of the personality tasks the golden mask dreamer did was to list a dozen different masks she wore—all of the different roles or functions that were part of her past and present repertoire. When she completed the list, she was asked to put the letter E next to all those masks that she could put on and take off easily; and the letter D next to those roles she found it difficult to put on or take off. Then she asked herself: "Which of these latter seem to encase me like the golden mask so that I can't seem to take them off?"

"The ones I found it very difficult to take off at will," she said, "were 'the good little girl always trying to please everyone' and 'mommy.' "

Here are her general comments on this technique:

> It was very helpful for me to move from the insights of issues about the mask to some concrete tasks. I needed to get my teeth into something real and practical, get some sense of control and movement. I made my lists. It was a relief to see things in writing. Finally, I had names for experiences and feelings that had been vague.
>
> I did have rights, for instance, and here on my list were five of them I wanted to exercise. I knew that if I was going to cease always being such a "nice girl," I was sometimes going to feel like a "bad girl" or even a "bitch."

*I needed plans to carry out these shifts in my behavior, to help me stay on track when I got scared or met the inevitable resistance to change, both within and without.*

*When I completed each task, I could own the success, chart my growth, keep feeding the energy with acknowledgment of my trying.*

*I took my tasks to my therapist for her acknowledgment and encouragement, for her suggestions, support, reflection, and insight. I was asking for help and getting it.*

*I remember a most powerful question my therapist asked, and I continued to ask myself, "Is it more important for you to be nice than to be healthy?" I had to re-choose my health—mental, physical, spiritual—on a daily basis.*

*After writing lists of choices and lists of affirmations, I would put them on the bathroom mirror where I had to face them and myself daily. I kept a journal of insights that produced more lists. All of this kept the symbol's energies alive.*

## TECHNIQUE 15: DO RELATIONSHIP TASKS

Relationship tasks are designed to bring the symbol's energies into your outer life, specifically to your relationships at work, at home, and at play. Using the symbol's energies in your relational life should begin to effect a transformation in the way you work, play, and love.

If you are doing symbol work with partners or a counselor, invite them to contribute to a list of outer life tasks that you might do to apply the symbol's energies in the ways you relate to people and the world in general.

Usually a list of six-to-ten suggestions is enough to give the dreamer a variety of tasks from which to choose. Remember, *the point is not to overwhelm the dreamer, but to see that the dreamer succeeds in keeping the symbol's energies alive in her life.*

If the relationship tasks your partners suggest do not possess the five qualities of a successful task, revise their suggestions in such a way that they do.

Here are some of the relationship tasks suggested to the mask dreamer:

Suggested Relationship Tasks

- Telephone two of the women you admire and affirm a quality in them that you admire.
- Within the next month, arrange a meeting (lunch or a walk) with two of the women on your "admire" list and discuss how they developed the qualities you admire.
- Choose one area from your list of areas where you need outside help and ask someone to help you, at least once.
- Accept a difficult job offer that would challenge you to act with assertiveness and confidence (the dreamer had just been offered such a position).
- Choose one course or workshop to take this year that has to do with assertiveness.
- During the next month, whenever you have your car serviced or some serviceperson comes to your house to repair something, ask the serviceperson to explain your bill as well as the service they performed.
- During the next month, at least once, when you think you haven't been treated fairly, confront the person and complain.

Of course, the dreamer did not do every one of these relationship tasks; on the other hand, she again developed and carried out other tasks not on this list. Because all of the suggested tasks possessed the five qualities of a good task, she experienced much success and kept the symbol energy alive in her life.

Here are some of her comments on this technique:

*I made a list of the women presently in my life that I admired. I listed the qualities about them I admired. I chose two and met with them and told them what I was doing and why they were on my list. I asked them how they had come by their qualities.*

*Janet, an artist, had a nude self-portrait on display in a show of women's self-portraits. I admired her acceptance of her own body and lack of embarrassment. I thought she had always been that way. She told me how she had struggled to get to this place. I discovered how alike we were, I felt less lonely, a new closeness. She explained to me some of the steps on her journey and I was encouraged and inspired.*

*Sarah, a lawyer, had many personal tragedies in her life, including divorce of parents, a child who committed suicide, and her own recent divorce. Yet Sarah seemed to be a high-spirited, productive, optimistic person. How did she manage? Sarah told me about how close to giving up she had felt at times, and how she would reground herself in meaningful work or study, how she counted on her friends and asked for their help. (When I took a vacation alone the next summer, it was Sarah who called me every day just to see how I was.)*

*An acquaintance was teaching an assertiveness course. I took his course, learned some very helpful, practical techniques and developed a wonderful, platonic relationship with an attractive man based on mutual admiration. To see that a man could really like my mind and not just my prettiness or sweetness was very affirming and remains a treasured and soul-satisfying relationship to this day.*

*All of the relationship tasks released energy in me, added momentum to my quest, carried me further, and opened up many new opportunities for growth. I didn't always know where I was on the journey but I did have my list and tasks to help me remain clear about where I was trying to go and the results I was seeking. And I was discovering some new ways of getting help and direction.*

## TECHNIQUE 16: LOOK FOR DREAMS THAT GIVE GUIDANCE AND CONFIRMATION

One way to find out if the symbol work you're doing is on track is to watch your dreams. Subsequent dreams often give guidance and confirmation to your dreamwork. Not all dreams do this, but some do. Usually, the dreams that do show a similarity to the dream with your chosen symbol.

One approach to this technique is directly to ask for a confirming dream. Just before you fall asleep, say to yourself that you want to dream a guidance dream about your symbol work. When you awake next morning, treat whatever dream you received as a source of guidance or confirmation about your symbol work.

Often, such dreams provide a special twist of wisdom that propel your dream task work in a certain direction. The dreamer of the mask dream had a number of such guidance dreams. Here are some of them, along with her comments and observations.

## CONFIRMING DREAM #1: SICK CANARY IN CAGE DREAM

The theme of the Sick Canary dream is similar to that of the Mask dream, a clear indication of the relationship.

*DREAM REPORT*

*I am in my house. I open a door and see a large room filled with bird cages. It is a bit like an aviary since there are plants around and lots of glass windows. However, I never knew this room was here and I have never tended the birds here. I am quite surprised to find the room. I notice the cage nearest me has a little female canary in it. Sitting on the bottom of the cage all ruffled up, she looks sick. I realize that though the cage has lots of food on its floor, the food is all fouled with bird droppings and the canary is being made sick by not having clean seed for healthy nourishment.*

*I realize all the cages must be in the same state and I am very upset at having forgotten and neglected this room full of birds. I again notice the little female canary in the cage nearest me and see how she is almost dead. I gently take her out of her cage and hold her in my hand. I cry and beg her to live, telling her I will clean her cage and give her good food and take care of her.*

Here are the dreamer's comments:

*I awoke from this dream with deep sadness and the anxiety that it might already be too late to save the dying canary.*

*A short time later, I told the dream to a woman gestalt therapist who guided me into a dialogue with the little canary. In the dialogue, I cried and begged the little bird to hold onto life. I said to the bird that I was aware of her need*

now, and I promised to take care of her. I told her how
sorry I was that she had been so neglected.

As in the golden mask dream, I was led to a room in my
house I didn't know existed. The theme of a neglected part
of me was clear. That this part was symbolized by a bird, a
spirit symbol in my Christian background, reminded me of
the neglect of my spiritual life. In earlier years I had found
comfort and hope, even nourishment, in spiritual practices. (Interestingly, the gestalt therapist was also an or-
dained minister.) I decided that this dream might be offering some encouragement to complement and support my
psychological growth with spiritual development.

## CONFIRMING DREAM #2: TOO-SWEET FISH TANK DREAM

After reflecting on the mask dream, the dreamer realized that
she had spent almost all of her life being sweet, too sweet in fact.
The need to put something into her life to balance her passive
sweetness was very clear, and her confirming dream was a strong
reminder not to forget that task.

### DREAM REPORT

I am in my house and there is a large fish tank, about four
feet wide and five feet tall. The fish are Blue Gills, like the
ones we caught while fishing in the Midwest lakes when I
was a child. The sunlight is pouring through the tank, and
to me it seems very beautiful. I do, however, notice tiny
bubbles all over the sides of the tank and the fish. A voice
tells me that the water is too sweet. I put a finger in and
taste the water, and it is indeed very sweet.

Here are the dreamer's comments:

I awake with a sense of discovery and insight. I realize I am
too sweet, I practically ooze sweetness. It is the word I
most often hear people use when talking about me. I know
I act sweetly and say Thank You, even when I am feeling
ripped off, irritated, angry, impatient, frustrated, etc. I am

also vaguely aware that my sweetness is reflected in my
"sweet life" as well, a life of many advantages and privi-
leges—and maybe that is not too healthy, either. Time to
change, but how to do it? What do I need?

## CONFIRMING DREAM #3: BITCH PUP DREAM

In reflecting on her personality tasks (Technique 14), the
dreamer had observed: "I knew that if I was going to cease always
being such a 'nice girl,' I was at times going to feel like a 'bad girl' or
even a 'bitch.' Using her own language, her inner self gave her a
dream that told her what she would need to deal with an environment that she had made too sweet.

*DREAM REPORT*

*I am in a barnyard looking at a bitch puppy, which I want to*
*take home for the family. My three daughters and husband*
*are with me. My husband doesn't like the puppy. He says*
*she is too dirty and he doesn't want "the little bitch" in the*
*house. I say that she's dirty only because she has been liv-*
*ing amid all that manure, but we can take her home and*
*clean her up. My husband doesn't want to, but I insist, "It*
*would be good for the girls to have her living with us."*
*And I add directly, "Besides, my daughters need the*
*little bitch."*

Here are the dreamer's comments:

*I awake with a sense of determination. I need to be more of*
*a bitch, less sweet and accommodating. Currently for me,*
*to be less than sweet means to be bitchy. My environment*
*at home won't be as sweet when this new "bitchy" ele-*
*ment is introduced, and I know I will feel my husband's*
*anger and resistance. Nevertheless, I know I must be more*
*assertive, as in the dream, and I must learn even to tolerate*
*my own anger and bitchiness. I know that, indeed, my*
*three bright, promising daughters need this dimension in*

*their lives if they are to grow up and be all they can be. All
of us "girls" need the "bitch."*

## CONFIRMING DREAM #4: PIG DREAM

This next confirming dream does precisely that. It confirms.
And it also clarifies one more dimension of the dreamer's new identity, a need for self-affirmation, some healthy pride in her own
accomplishments.

Once again, the resistance of husband and family members to
the dreamer's new emerging identity is noted.

*DREAM REPORT*

*I am again in a barnyard with my family and I notice a little
pig. The pig keeps trying to get our attention by showing
off. The little pig is standing on its head, but at the same
time it is defecating. It is funny to watch this little pig, and
it does attract our attention.*

Here are the dreamer's comments on this confirming dream:

*I awoke feeling guilty. I wonder why? For showing off? For
wanting attention? I realized my husband often referred to
things I did that he didn't like as "shitty." I usually felt that
to want something for myself was to be "piggish" (selfish).
Once when I was a kid, my mother insisted that I give away
some paper dolls that I treasured. When I resisted, she told
me that I was acting selfishly, being a pig. If what I wanted
to hold onto today would make my husband unhappy, how
selfish and shitty of me.*

*Was I also being a bitch by holding onto something I
wanted for me? I wanted the bitch puppy as part of my
wholeness. What did this mean in practical terms? It meant
I wanted to get my Ph.D. and I wanted to make a noticeable
difference in the world, especially regarding children. Ulti-
mately, I wanted attention and appreciation for my efforts.
To achieve all this would require that I take time for myself. On the other hand, my husband had told me that time
not spent with him was time taken from him. It was clear*

*that to continue on this path would be seen (By whom? Me?
My husband? My children? The world?) as selfish, shitty of
me—and owning the bitch.*

## CONFIRMING DREAM #5: THE GIANT GOLDFISH
## AND THE SHARK

As the dreamer begins to do personality tasks and relationship
tasks that express her new-found assertive (bitchy) energies, the
outer world becomes a scary place. What is she to do with the good
little baby girl (the poor canary, the sweet fish) if she brings into her
environment a screaming child imprisoned in a mask, a bitch
puppy, and a shitty pig? How can they possibly live together? Won't
they cause chaos and destroy the present environment? What is the
cost, and is she equipped to pay it? It is a real fear.

*DREAM REPORT*

> *I am looking at a very large aquarium, as in a museum. The
> water is murky so I cannot see the fish. Then, out of the
> murkiness swims a giant goldfish, like Cleo in Pinocchio.
> She has long eyelashes and a long fantail, very sweet, femi-
> nine-looking, seductive-acting, swishing her tail around
> and batting her eyelashes. She disappears into the murki-
> ness and then, suddenly and unexpectedly, a huge shark
> appears. It is vicious-looking and menacing in its move-
> ments. It also swims back into the murkiness. I am terrified
> by the realization that both fish are in the tank and I don't
> know which will appear. I wonder if the shark will devour
> the sweet and harmless pretty goldfish.*

These are her comments after reflecting on the shark dream:

> *I awoke filled with fear and anxiety. The questions posed
> by the dream are vivid in my mind and easily translatable:
> Which part of me will appear next, the sweet and harmless
> goldfish or the vicious and destructive shark? Will the
> "shadow," shark side of me kill off the sweet "persona"
> side of me? I am reminded that my astrological sign is*

> *Pisces, the two fish. Both live in me. I am obviously attracted by the goldfish and terrified by the shark in me, a true statement of my feelings.*

## FURTHER RESEARCH AND SYMBOL WORK ON THE GOLDEN MASK

In further research of the mask as a symbol, the dreamer turned to J.E. Cirlot's *A Dictionary of Symbols* where the primary symbolic meaning of mask was given as *transformation*. Cirlot wrote:

> All transformations are invested with something at once of profound mystery and of the shameful, since anything that is so modified as to become "something else" while still remaining the thing that it was, must inevitably be productive of ambiguity and equivocation. Therefore, metamorphoses must be hidden from view—and hence the need for the mask. Secrecy tends towards transfiguration: it helps what-one-is to become what-one-would-like-to-be; and this is what constitutes its magic character . . . (pp. 195–96).

The dreamer could easily see the truth of the mask as a symbol of transformation. First, there was the transformation that must have happened to the child during the period it was encased in the golden mask. But there would also be a second transformation of the child after the mask was removed.

The new element of the symbol that Cirlot brought into focus for the dreamer—the shameful quality of a mask—was one she had missed in amplifying the symbol (Technique 4). "Does wearing the golden mask occasion an experience of shame?" became a question for reflection.

The dreamer also found it helpful to meditate on the metamorphosis she herself was going through that "must be hidden from view." Much of her therapeutic work and the inner life tasks she was performing to keep alive the energy of the major dream of the golden mask would be hidden from view.

Thanks to Cirlot's observations, she also reflected on the question: "In what ways did the golden mask dream also symbolize for me not only something I want to remove but, as Cirlot put it, what-one-would-like-to-be?'' An important personality task she did was to list the ways the golden mask and the child within it symbolized what she would like to be. She found it rather easy to list the ways the child in the golden mask symbolized what she was at the time, but paradoxical to think that the golden mask symbol could be a harbinger of what was to come. Cirlot gave her some hints.

A secondary symbolic meaning of mask, according to Cirlot, was that "the mask, simply as a face, comes to express the solar and energetic aspects of the life-process" (p. 196).

At first, this secondary meaning seemed to find little or no resonance in the dreamer's mind, until she read Cirlot's entry under "gold," where he wrote"

> Gold is the image of solar light and hence of the divine intelligence. If the heart is the image of the sun in man, in the earth it is gold. Consequently, gold is symbolic of all that is superior. . . . Everything golden tends to pass on this quality of superiority to its utilitarian function (p. 114).

Thus, a golden sword would possess a quality of superiority over a sword made of any other metal. In the myth, Chrysaor, the magic sword of gold, symbolizes supreme spiritual determination.

In Alexandre Dumas' novel *The Man in the Iron Mask,* the mask was made of iron, a baser metal. The mask on the child in her dream was of gold, and therefore symbolic of all that is superior and spiritual. The dreamer commented:

> *From my other readings in symbolism, I had learned that gold speaks to the transpersonal, the spiritual, the divine. Was there some aspect of the mask that was concerned with God? Was my dream meant to be more than just my personal dream? Did it have some larger significance? Would others be touched by it?*
>
> *The features on the golden mask were generic rather than specific, the mask did not have its own unique personality. Transpersonal things did not have their own personality because they spoke to all humankind. Was my mask dream speaking to more than me?*

If the mask is a symbol of transfiguration—Cirlot said, "The mask is equivalent to the chrysalis" (p. 196)—then a golden mask hints at a superior and spiritual transfiguration. To what kind of transformation was she being invited, she wondered.

As if to underline her awareness and question, Cirlot continued:

> Gold is also the essential element in the symbolism of the hidden or elusive treasure which is an illustration of the fruits of the spirit and of supreme illumination (pp. 114–15).

Not only was the dreamer's mask made of gold, it was also a work of art, probably worthy of being displayed in a museum. Thus, if Cirlot was correct, not only does the mask symbolize an illumination of the divine spirit but also symbolizes the best of the creative human spirit that made it a work of art.

The dreamer wondered what this symbolism could mean, since the mask in the dream, if not removed, would indeed soon kill the life of the undernourished child imprisoned in it. Could divine illumination and human artistry be aimed at death and destruction?

At this point, on a hunch, she looked up "twins" in Cirlot's *A Dictionary of Symbols* and discovered that "twins" generally signify two essential but different aspects of a thing. Sometimes twins symbolize life and death, light and darkness, white and black, day and night, consciousness and unconsciousness. Sometimes, like the sun, twins symbolize appearance and disappearance; sometimes, like mountains and valleys, one twin represents heaven and the other earth; sometimes one twin may be a peaceful shepherd, the other a fierce hunter. Often one twin represents the celestial or spiritual side, the other the mortal side. Sometimes twins "symbolize the counterbalancing principles of good and evil, and hence the twins are portrayed as mortal enemies" (p. 337).

As the dreamer read Cirlot's entry under "twins," key questions began to tumble out of her mind.

- *Are the twins in my dream somehow mortal enemies?*
- *Is it possible that the good little girl asleep could be antagonistic to the child in the golden mask?*
- *Which child in the dream symbolizes consciousness?*
- *Could the mask be a life-giving force to the child and to me?*
- *Was the child in the mask also a symbol of spiritual growth?*
- *Was the golden mask put on the child by the divine spirit?*

■ *Is it likely that fruits of the spirit and divine illumination would come to me via the mask and the dreamwork I did with the symbol?*

Some personality tasks also suggested themselves:

■ *List at least five ways the two children are different or possess contrasting qualities.*
■ *List at least three ways the golden mask and the child in it symbolize "what-one-is."*
■ *List at least three ways the golden mask and the child in it symbolize "what-one-would-like-to-be."*
■ *Note three ways the golden mask is like a chrysalis.*
■ *Note one or two ways the golden mask possesses the qualities of superiority and spirituality.*
■ *List four or five ways in which the golden mask has produced spiritual illumination in me.*

Inspired by her research, her key questions, and her personality tasks, the dreamer carried out some dreamwork comparing the two children: the good little girl fast asleep and the crying child in the golden mask—first, with the mask on and, then, with the mask off.

*I made a balance sheet. First, I listed the qualities I recognized in the first child asleep in the nursery: sweet, feminine, pretty, quiet, non-threatening, cooperative, lovable, charming, easily satisfied, cuddly, kissable, desirable. People liked being around her and wanted to hold her. She was ideal.*

*Next, I characterized the child in the golden mask as: frightening, strange, out-of-place, shameful, guilt-producing to others, unable to see or hear well, unable to hold its head up, utterly isolated and alone, unsocialized, its brain and mind distorted. This child threatened the ego of others, made others aware of their neglect of it and their irresponsibility. The child in the mask was unable to live interpersonally and had not been introduced to the larger world. The golden headscarf, which I learned about only by carrying the symbol backward in time, was the only fragment of the mother to which the child had bonded.*

*Was this a symbol of the superior qualities of the head—
intellect, wisdom, spirit—which I had inherited from my
mother?*

*Finally, I tried to characterize the child with the mask
removed. I realized that it would look ugly for a long time.
Its skin would be dry, chafed, wrinkled, colorless, and require a lot of careful tending. It would have to be fed very
slowly and carefully. It would need to be changed, bathed,
and caressed. Touched. It would need lots of tactile
stimulation.*

When she carried forward the symbol of the child in the golden
mask, after the mask was removed, she discovered that the child had
no personality of its own. The child was undernourished, underde-
veloped. She thought of putting the two children together, but that
would be a future dreamwork task.

*I became aware that freed from the constraints of the mask
the child would be able to cry, laugh, and play. The child
would hear and see things. And with that, it would begin
expressing its needs and possibly become demanding. At
first, the child would be easily confused, easily frightened,
easily overstimulated. It would not know who were its family and friends, and who weren't. And whom to trust. It
would need to learn to hold its head up and other behav-
iors appropriate to its age.*

*At different times, I tried to carry the symbol of the
child forward to see if it was male or female. Sometimes the
child seemed to be a girl, the identical twin, one egg that
had split and reflected the original wholeness. At other
times the child seemed to be a boy, the masculine counterpart twin reflecting the wholeness of the opposites united.
Both images seemed true because, for each, wholeness was
the key.*

## AFTER TWELVE YEARS OF SYMBOL WORK ON THE GOLDEN MASK (THE DREAMER'S WORDS)

Nearly a dozen years have passed since I first experienced and
told my golden mask dream at the Florida colloquium. I've done

symbol work on the original dream numerous times, at first because I felt I needed to unlock its meaning and energy, but then at least several times a year in later years as part of classes in dreamwork. Students in courses or workshops have replaced the original group of listeners and have experienced the symbol techniques with me. Each student group has presented me with new insights, and uncovered some new dimension of the golden mask symbol.

None of the original insights have been discarded, more have been added. The symbol's meaning and power have expanded, more and more energy and depth of understanding have been released.

What has happened to me over these dozen years? How have I lived out the truth of this dream?

I spent many of those years in therapy with a highly skilled professional who used a variety of therapeutic tools in helping remove the mask. My therapist clearly identified removing the mask as her task in our first session, and reminded me during our final session that this had always been our task. She was also a wise and nurturing mother, gentle, caring, and sensitive. I have no doubt that she did and always will love me, and that she saw the worst as well as the best of me and deeply loved the whole person.

I did finish my Ph.D. and was licensed in clinical psychology. I specialized for many years in work with children, especially abused and deprived children. I co-authored a book with Louis Savary called *Building Self-Esteem in Children* from my experiences with children.

Louis Savary was my partner at the mask-making workshop. It was the first time I had met him. His sensitivity and gentle touch produced the beautiful mask I could hold in my own hands. Lou has continued to be my partner, as he was in the workshop, encouraging me to see the potential that I hold in my hands, co-creating with me, and inviting me to do the same for him.

My safe and peaceful world did end up in chaos. My old, secure lifestyle with its focus upon beautiful houses, elegant entertaining, and an ideal-looking family came to an end. My marriage ended, ties were broken, my children were confused, I was confused. My environment did indeed become less sweet.

Almost twenty years before, my husband had married me, had contracted for a life with the good little girl, pretty, sweet, serene, and asleep (unconscious). He wanted me to continue to be the person he had married, and I realized he hadn't married a person but a mask. And I wanted to be a real person. In many ways, my children also wanted me to keep the sweet mask on. They wanted me to continue to be the mother that had made them the envy of their friends, always giving, always adaptable, never angry or needy.

When the mask came off, I think we all saw the unmasked child-woman as ugly.

Slowly, I built more real relationships with my daughters. We became whole, complex people relating to each other. I discovered, just as I had worn the mask of being nice and good, I had expected them to do so also. But the good little girl masks dropped away from all of us, and we struggled with real love, real acceptance and, for me at least, real patience, commitment, and trust. The relationships that emerged among us all were deeply loving and wise, open and generous, trusting and vulnerable, loyal and confident. This alone has been worth the whole process/journey.

Sometimes I wondered, if I had known ahead of time the cost, the anxiety, the sense of loss, the uncovering of the abused and deprived child I had actually been, and the mourning that entailed, the sadness and the fear, would I have chosen the process?

I know I did make it more difficult for myself by being fearful. I went along my path kicking and screaming. It would have been better if I had been like the child in my waking dream and been so caught up in the goldsmith's work that I wasn't frightened. Indeed, to the extent that I could recognize the healthiness of the process either from my own professional knowledge or that of my therapist, I was comforted and more at peace.

The process is not over. I am still struggling to establish a balance in my life. I'm still trying to integrate receiving and assertiveness, rights and requesting, defending and surrender. I'm still trying to grasp that the life I am living is *my* life, my journey and my responsibility, and to enjoy it as an adventure rather than as something to get through as safely as possible. My childhood woundedness will probably always be with me, hopefully not crippling me but adding to my compassion and complexity, part of the real me to enrich my work and my world.

I thought I had lost so much when my world, as I perceived it, broke up along with my marriage. I hated the pain I had brought into the family and the terrible loss of security. In time, I gained back so much more than was lost and with it the capacity to feel and enjoy intensely. Working with my dreams was crucial to this reclaiming of life for me.

Today, much of my clinical work is helping what I call "women in transition," other women struggling to remove masks, to overcome the wounds of abuse, to develop wholeness, to be their true selves.

It has been twelve years since I walked into a small efficiency unit on the campus of that small Florida college where I first had the dream of the child in the golden mask. On arrival, I can remember having a heady sense of "All my own space, just mine, for a whole month!" I had greedily insisted on a singles accommodation for myself.

At the same time I was also thinking, "What am I doing here? My husband and three children are at home. I left before the Christmas tree was taken down!" I remember smiling to myself in having arranged such a clever escape from that chore which I disliked. And in the next breath I said to myself, "They will never forgive me," and felt guilt at my delight.

At the time, I also felt some strange sense of threat. My first night in that apartment, I put a chair in front of the door for protection.

The threat to my safety and security came several nights later, but not from outside my door. The power that changed my life forever came from within. How do you protect yourself from being visited by a dream whose time has come?

For the past dozen years, I have shared my personal private space with this unbidden intruder, which I have named my "Mask Dream." Since I believe that dreams also belong to the community, I now give this dream to you. I put it on display in this public place. Maybe it will speak to you in some healing way. Maybe it will bring something of beauty and value into your life and release transforming energies in you.

## Part II

Spirituality
and
Dreams

# Chapter 4
# *SPIRITUALITY AND WHOLENESS*

## WIDESPREAD INTEREST IN SPIRITUAL GROWTH

In psychological and psychiatric circles today, there is much interest in spirituality. The interface between psychology and spirituality has stirred up much interest at recent psychiatric meetings. For instance, recently in Washington, The Psychiatric Institute held a conference on spirituality which attracted one of the largest professional audiences in the Institute's history. Also, the Association for Humanistic Psychology at its regional meetings traditionally divides conference participants into various interest groups. For a number of years, spirituality has been included as an interest category, and it invariably draws the largest crowd. Recently established and headquartered in Washington is a young and rapidly growing organization called Common Boundary, whose "common boundary" is the intersection of psychology and spirituality. Its membership has doubled each year since it began.

As technicians and artisans of the psychological spiritual, we explore in this book the ways persons interested in holistic growth may look at dreams and the symbols that appear in them. Our focus in this section is spirituality.

## THE MEANING AND STRUCTURE OF SPIRITUALITY

Despite widespread interest in spirituality, there is much vagueness and fuzziness about what *spirituality* means. What is its domain? Its function? How, for example, does it differ from psychology? Or from religion?

At one extreme, some people equate spirituality with institutional religion. For them, spiritual practice is simply reciting prayers, attending worship, listening to sermons, meditating or singing sacred hymns. At the other extreme, some equate spirituality with occult and superstitious practices. Such people might put into

71

this category everything that seems weird to them: from Ouija boards, crystal balls, tarot cards, and voodoo dolls all the way to clairvoyance, psychic healing, channeling, and out-of-body experience. Technically speaking, the domain of the spiritual doesn't exclude any of these practices or experiences. From the most traditional monk in his monastery to the most occult alchemist in his laboratory, people are operating in the domain of the human spirit and utilizing energy that is available to that spirit.

It is not an easy task to define *spirituality*. Many years ago, when in our workshops we dealt primarily with Roman Catholics, mostly priests and sisters, it was easy to define spirituality as "my relationship with Jesus Christ and his church."

About a dozen years ago, however, when we first joined the adjunct faculty at the Pacific School of Religion in Berkeley, the students were more ecumenical. As we welcomed Sufis, Buddhists, Hindus, and Taoists as well as many different denominations of Christians into our classes, we had to broaden our definition of spirituality to "my relationship to God."

But, in recent years, as spirituality began to attract an even broader range of people, we would find in our workshops people interested in spirituality who didn't belong to any church and some who didn't even believe in God. "We have a human spirit," they would say to us, "so we are interested in spirituality."

This forced us to deal with the realization that religion and spirituality are not equivalent terms, though they are often used interchangeably by theologians and church people. So, when we spoke about spirituality, we needed to make that distinction clear. And it's a basically simple distinction. Religion has to do with what pertains to the church, while spirituality has to do with what pertains to the human spirit. When the human spirit attends church and operates from within a church framework or a certain theology, religion and spirituality naturally intersect.

But, as some of our students made clear to us, religious experience doesn't, and in fact cannot, contain everything that the human spirit experiences. Certainly, almost anyone could list dozens of experiences of the human spirit, such as philosophy, drama, art, music, creativity, friendship, healing, altruism, commitment to a cause, humor, etc., that are not necessarily connected with religion or some church.

In this broader sense, the dreamer's story of her golden mask dream and symbol work is a story of dreams and spirituality.

*Working on the dream revealed to me that my self-image might be described as "a work of art only surface deep." Since the goldsmith considered the mask a work of art, I expected people wanted to see only the pretty, outer level of me. After doing symbol work on the dream, I realized I was going to have to find my own depth, to deal with the many levels of me that were behind the mask.*

When the dreamer first told the mask dream at the Florida colloquium, someone had asked her, "The mask is such a beautiful work of art, are you sure you don't want to leave it on?"

"A human child is far more beautiful than any work of art," the dreamer quickly replied, "and I have the twin child in the next room to prove it." She knew the spiritual truth about the innate beauty and inherent value of every human being, no matter what its defects. Affirming the beauty and value of each person, independent of any religious doctrines, is an element of every spiritual journey.

## A DEFINITION FOR EVERYONE

Our challenge was to find a definition of spirituality that differentiated spirituality from religion, but did not exclude it: a definition that would work for everyone, and around which everyone could talk.

We finally found a way of defining spirituality that we think will work for everyone. It is this. *Spirituality is my way of being, acting, relating, thinking, and choosing in light of my ultimate values.*

If you happen to be a devout Christian for whom Jesus, God, the church, and the Ten Commandments are among your ultimate values, then you can use this definition of spirituality. On the other hand, if you don't believe in God and give meaning to your life primarily by adhering to certain ultimate values such as love, truth, freedom, equality or women's rights, then this definition of spirituality fits you, too.

According to this definition, everyone who has a human spirit has a spirituality. Your spirituality may be conscious or unconscious. It may be healthy or destructive. It may be clear or confused. It may be simple or complex. But it is operating. And part of our work as technicians of the spiritual is helping people bring their spirituality to the light of consciousness.

Doing symbol work on the mask dream forced the dreamer to struggle with her ultimate values, in naming them and coming to terms with them.

During most of her life before the dream, her ultimate values had been: Security, Being Taken Care Of, Being Loved, and Being Good. According to her beliefs, as her reward for being good, helpful, lovable, nice, sweet, flexible, adaptable, uncomplaining, never angry, never having opinions of her own, always being there for her husband or the children, etc., she would be taken care of and feel secure.

In the mask dream, this value system was symbolized by the good little baby who was cute and sweet and didn't cause any trouble. Clearly, this good little girl had received her reward. She was well taken care of, well-dressed, well-fed, loved, secure. She was getting her needs met.

But the other child obviously was not. The needy, hungry, undernourished, uncared-for, angry, ugly and complaining baby in the mask, who was insecure to the point of deprivation and near death, challenged the dreamer to reflect on ultimate values symbolized by the child in the golden mask.

> *The dream and its dreamwork put me in touch with wanting to be whole, to be grown up, to be responsible, to be helpful, to make a contribution to the world. To hold these new ultimate values, I could still be a loving and giving person, but I needed to be more. I would have to take risks. To make a difference in the world, I would need to discover and develop my talents, to claim my identity, and to explore those areas where I might make a contribution. Like the baby who wanted to get out of the mask, I'd have to be able to tolerate making trouble, upsetting people, causing a stir, confronting others' opinions and expectations of me with my own views and needs.*
>
> *In the dream, the sweet little girl was asleep. Like her, I seem to have been asleep for many years. I don't want to*

*be asleep any longer. I want to be awake, aware, conscious.*
*I don't want to distort and waste my mind the way my*
*mother unconsciously did. I want to choose consciousness*
*over the comforts of oblivion.*
*I want to know who I am and why I'm the way I am.*
*Discovering the answers to such questions would become*
*a major part of my task in studying clinical psychology.*

It was difficult for the dreamer to make the choice for wholeness and consciousness because she soon discovered things she
didn't like about herself and her life.

*I didn't like knowing that I hadn't been the perfect mother.*
*In trying to get my daughters always to be nice, as I was, I*
*had given them some unhealthy messages. I had told them*
*that being good girls—being nice, sweet, agreeable, and*
*having people like you—was the most important thing,*
*when in fact being "a good little girl" was not a healthy*
*ultimate value upon which to base their lives and goals.*
*I didn't like discovering how important my own com-*
*fort was to me. I had thought all along that I was altruistic*
*and willing to undergo any amount of discomfort for what I*
*believed in, but it just wasn't true.*
*I didn't like finding out that I was afraid of making*
*people angry. I would rather have described myself as flex-*
*ible and adaptable, but it was really a disguised fear of*
*confrontation.*
*I didn't like finding out I was indecisive. I would*
*rather have described myself as easy to please or easy to get*
*along with, but it was really a disguise for fear of*
*disapproval.*

Even before the mask dream, the dreamer had already begun to
shift her ultimate values. Choosing to enter the Ph.D. program itself
forced her to take time for herself. Choosing to participate in the
month-long colloquium in Florida forced her to take time away from
the family. Choosing to prepare herself academically and clinically
forced her to develop herself, do research, and put academic needs
before other traditional family obligations for a time. She was going

against her values of being a nice person and always available to her family. "My family were already resenting it," she said, "and I could feel their resentment."

Another doctoral candidate, a friend of hers, asked her if they could share a room at the Florida colloquium, but she said, "No, I need the privacy and time for myself." Saying No was quite unlike her. Once again, she was moving away from her old value of always being flexible and adaptable.

She was becoming conscious of another dimension of herself when she arrived at the colloquium, and the dream reflected the fact that this forgotten part of her was making itself heard in the cries of the masked child.

> *This newly discovered part of me was alive, awake, making an impact on my life and others as well. The dream was inviting me to consider the ultimate value of wholeness— of bringing together body, mind, and spirit.*

Some months later, she had a dream which challenged her to acknowledge that she had shifted her ultimate values from Safety and Security and Being Loved to Giving Love.

> *In the dream I had a dialogue with a voice, which I took to be my inner Self or God. It went like this:*

Voice: *"What is the biggest wish of your life?"*
Me:     *"To be loved." (This had been the theme of my childhood, what I had always wanted.)*
Voice: *"Aren't you loved?"*
Me:     *"Yes, I am. I am loved by my children, many friends, my students and clients."*
Voice: *"So, are you loved?"*
Me:     *"Yes."*
Voice: *"So, what is now the biggest wish of your life?"*
Me:     *"To love."*

> *In the dream, I realized that I had a new ultimate value —to be able to love and give love—and because of it I was*

*growing free of the driving need to feel loved. I could be*
*free to focus on being a giver of love as well as a receiver.*

## SPIRITUALITY AND STYLE

People who have little awareness of the spiritual dimension at work in their lives often confuse spirituality with personal style. Spirituality and style are two different concepts, even though they both have to do with one's way of being and acting in daily life, and might therefore *seem* similar.

There is an essential difference between the two concepts. While *spirituality* is my way of being and acting in light of my ultimate values, *style* is my way of being and acting in light of my everyday, operating values. Some everyday, operating values include: *cleanliness, clarity, organization, friendliness, fashion, spontaneity, good humor, punctuality, good taste, honesty.*

In practice, the two—spirituality and style—are frequently confused, because in translating your ultimate values into everyday behavior that behavior is naturally carried out in your own style. Powerful dreams avoid this confusion and are able to reveal ultimate values with clarity.

> *In another dream, my daughter Evie and I were in prison. We and everyone with us were sentenced to death. Instead of taking me, they called my daughter first. I realized I loved her so much that I wouldn't allow them to take her. As I held her in my arms, I let out an incredible, roaring scream that came up from my toes and freed up an enormous amount of energy within me. With that energy, I tore away a big, upright support pillar in the room and broke down the door with it. I took her to safety and was followed by the other prisoners.*
>
> *Imprisonment recalled the old, familiar mask theme. The dream was telling me that I was accepting the gifts of courage and strength to lead my children and my clients to an inner freedom.*
>
> *In another dream about the same daughter, I had left her to wait on a float upon the ocean during the night while I swam to shore to get help. When I returned with help, I couldn't find her. Certain she had drowned, I was grief-*

*stricken, not just that she had died but that she had died
alone. Alone! How awful! My worst fear, to face terror and
death alone. I would rather have stayed and died with her
than to let her die alone without me.*

*This dream reflected the tremendous value I place on
relationships and bonds of love. It also spoke to my fear of
dying without being connected to myself and the child
within. It reflected my wish not to abandon a part of me to
die—symbolized by a child of mine, as in the golden
mask dream.*

## SOMETHING MUCH MORE CONSEQUENTIAL

What you decide and do influenced by your ultimate values is
something much more consequential than the clothes you choose,
the music you listen to, the kind of food you eat, the friends you
prefer. Your ultimate values ask you questions such as: "What am I
doing on this planet?" "Why am I here?" "What is my meaning and
purpose?" "What am I contributing to the human community?"
"What does life and death mean to me?" "What does wholeness,
health, truth, beauty, freedom, relationship mean to me?" "To what
am I truly committed?" "What would I give up my life for?" "Or,
more practically, for what goal would I live my life?" These are
spirituality questions.

For the dreamer, the major effects of the dreamwork began to
show in shifts in her ultimate values. From her ultimate value of
comfort she began a shift to development of her whole self; from
being loved, to loving; from security, to truth and courage.

At times, these shifts required some adventure, daring, and risk-
taking on her part.

*In my academic development, I began going after what I
really wanted. A chaplain I knew at Georgetown University
Hospital mentioned that the hospital was offering a medical ethics course dealing with, among other topics, Karen
Ann Quinlan, a young New Jersey woman in a permanent
coma who was being kept alive only by respirators, with no
hope of ever regaining consciousness. I was interested in
the ethical, spiritual, and psychological issues involved for
my family and the professional staff where I worked. So I*

*approached the professor, an action I would never have
dared in my old value system, and asked if I could join his
class. Even though I was not enrolled in the university
there, nor was I on the hospital staff, I told him I wanted to
do it as part of my Ph.D. program. He said yes.*

The ethics professor saw her as someone truly committed to
what she wanted and to exploring important life issues. She was not
choosing the seminar as an expression of her style, but of her ultimate values—her desire to be awake, conscious, whole.

In her new value system she was able to (1) *identify something
she really wanted,* such as the information and experience that
would come from the medical ethics course; (2) *be assertive
enough to request it or go after it,* such as asking the professor for
permission to attend; and (3) *present herself as qualified to have
the result.* Here, she spoke to the professor in ways that showed her
as an intelligent, serious, and capable professional with confidence
in and ownership of her qualities. Indeed, the professor saw her as
an appropriate participant of his seminar.

## CLARIFYING ULTIMATE VALUES

In spirituality, clarifying your ultimate values is a major, ongoing process, both for individuals and groups. For example, many
churches prescribe or assign certain ultimate values as part of their
belief structures and, consequently, these values are given to their
followers. Still, individuals and even the churches themselves as
institutions are called upon almost continually to clarify the meaning of those ultimate values, perhaps to modify them and to reorga-
nize or re-hierarchize them, and of course always to make choices,
decisions, policies, plans, strategies, and schedules based on those
values. Clarifying ultimate values is an adult's task, not a child's. The
dreamer became aware of how the ultimate values she currently
held were probably implanted in her during childhood.

*As a Catholic child, I recognized that ultimate values were
prescribed for me. My parochial school and religious upbringing made it very clear what the church wanted from
me. So did my parents. What was right and what was wrong
were spelled out in detail. The main value was that one*

should be good. *This meant that long-suffering was good and complaining was bad; martyrdom was good and anger was bad; obedience was good and rebellion was bad; giving was better than receiving, and a lot of giving and no receiving was even better. Somewhere in all of this came the rule: Silence is golden. This meant, among other things: Never complain. Never ask for things because wanting is self-centered, selfish, and greedy. Pain is to be quietly endured and "offered up," rather than tended to; this meant you were expected to be brave, silent, and long-suffering as well as good.*

*In my child's mind I may have distorted the church's true meaning of virtue, but I was sure no one had ever asked me to define what it meant to be good. Goodness was defined for me. It was prescribed much like a formula—or a role. It was not presented, to me at least, as a consciously thought-out and chosen way to live.*

*My mask dream brought out a different way of looking at the child's anger, crying out, wanting, complaining, asking for attention and care. This child was crying out for the necessities of existence itself. And I could see that, again and again in my life, I had kept silent when I had every right to cry out for the necessities I was not getting from my family and from my church.*

*I have come to learn that the founder of Christianity was much more in favor of wholeness than I was ever led to believe. That founder said, "I came that you may have life and have it more abundantly." For example, if I happened to develop a painful disease, I would seek both to have the best possible care taken of myself and try not to be a complainer. My primary purpose, however, would be to fully nurture my strength and use it.*

*I have shifted in my view of women's roles, too. Traditionally, women were seen as nurturers to children, companions to their husbands, good little girls to their parents, and hard-working, obedient women to the church. Women weren't thought of as taking the hero's journey. Their role was to nurture rather than earn money, to be protected rather than defend, to adapt rather than to take risks, to support others rather than innovate.*

But now I see the hero's journey as transcending gender, because the hero's journey is really the best way to describe the development of the human soul. The hero's journey is precisely the spiritual journey.

## VALUES AS LIVING THINGS

For each of us, ultimate values are very living things and profoundly influence our lives.

Ask yourself what ultimate value you rank first in your life. Some perennially top values include: money, power, security, survival, social advancement, being liked and respected, pleasure, true friendship, salvation, world peace, equality, research, freedom, etc.

For the dreamer of the mask dream, safety and security had been ultimate values, but in a very unique way.

*Though I experienced safety and security as an adult, they were absent from my childhood. I'm sure I always wanted them; it's just that they were not provided. What I experienced instead was lack of protection, lack of physical care, and unpredictable abuse.*

*Throughout my life, from childhood—and even after my mother died—I tended to treat myself the way my mother treated me, as if my health and life were unimportant.*

*Once when I was sixteen, I had a strep throat infection for two weeks during the Christmas vacation, and my mother didn't notice that I was sick, not eating, and losing weight. The day I went back to school, I looked so badly that my friends didn't recognize me. On the following day before I left for school, I collapsed on the floor. That's when my mother called the doctor. The doctor said that my throat had gotten so bad that if it weren't for penicillin, I probably would have died in a few days.*

*However, my mother's concern had not been that I stay alive and healthy, but that I was costing money. She* was furious that my illness was forcing her to spend money for the doctor. I was sad when I realized her ultimate value was saving money. As a consequence, being safe and secure in my own childhood home could not be counted on, so these values became a preoccupation with me in later life, and so did my family value of saving money. Valuing myself was not something I learned to do in childhood. It was something I still needed to learn.

As a child, when I was abused by my mother, the most dangerous thing I could do would be to try to defend myself. If I tried that, as I did a few times, she would become even more enraged. So, I learned not to defend myself. Now I needed to learn how and when to defend myself.

During the times I was being beaten by my mother, I was told not to make a sound lest the neighbors hear me cry. She did not want the neighbors to know she was beating me. To ensure my silence, she would often stuff a sock in my mouth. So, I learned that crying out or asking for help were not ways to take care of myself. Expressing my pain and standing up for my rights was something I still needed to learn. I was living as though I still had a sock in my mouth.

The child in the mask, however, was crying out for help, letting the world know about the abuse, deprivation, and neglect it was experiencing. Everything in my childhood pattern revolted against crying out for help or in complaint. The child in the mask crying out was new to me. The dream was suggesting new ways for me to behave if I wanted to become a whole person who was fully alive.

I realize that my ultimate values of safety and security were not freely chosen from a list of ultimate values. For every human being, safety and security are fundamental human needs, almost as basic as food, clothing, and a roof over one's head. These fundamental needs never got fulfilled in my childhood.

Other children might have enjoyed safety and security in childhood, and in adult life might still freely choose them as ultimate values, as a way to get through life without facing challenges or taking risks. I had to choose them *because* I never had them in childhood. *My human nature still required safety and security before it could grow and become whole.*

## ULTIMATE VALUES INFLUENCE THE WHOLE PERSON

Each of these ultimate values, whichever they may be for you, touches your whole life. They influence your physical life and how you use your body; they influence your psychological life and how you use your mind and emotions; they influence your human spirit and how you use your spiritual capacities. In short, they influence your whole person.

To describe the whole person, we use the ordinary definition: the unity of body, mind, and spirit. These three domains of the human person are fully integrated in reality. Whenever you do any action, the three domains participate in that action. Only the mind can think and talk about the body, mind, and spirit separately, and that's what people often do. For instance, no one would challenge you if you said a person could be physically healthy but psychologically ill, or vice versa. Similarly, you probably know someone currently who is both physically healthy and spiritually sick, or vice versa.

The body, mind, and spirit each have different requirements and preferences. While the body needs vitamins and exercise and the mind needs to feed on thought and communication, the spirit needs to find meaning and purpose in life. Nevertheless, all of the domains are really always meant to operate as a unity in service to the whole person.

Values are very important in spirituality. Sometimes people's ranking of ultimate values is dysfunctional or harmful, as when a person is destined to create important things in this lifetime but is totally absorbed in making money or climbing the corporate power ladder. When this happens, the deepest self is likely to reveal that discrepancy between destiny and current behavior in the person's dreams. Dreaming, just like every other natural human function, is for our health and wholeness.

Dreams can reflect your spirituality: the way you think and act in light of your ultimate values. Dreams can reflect your spirituality holistically: they can tell you how you are using your body and its physical energies, how you are using your mind and emotions and their psychological energies, and how you are using your human spirit and its spiritual energies. Clarification of the values being revealed by the dream is the task of dreamwork. From the perspective of spirituality, dreams provide holistic data in metaphoric form for the choices that the waking ego will be called upon to make.

## Chapter 5
# PREMISES ABOUT DREAMS
# AND SPIRITUALITY

### SOME PREMISES OF DREAMS AND SPIRITUALITY

We have articulated ten basic premises, or assumptions, about dreams and dreamwork that connect dreams and spirituality. They are derived from our perspective as technicians of the spiritual.

Many of you may study dreams from the perspective of another discipline, e.g., as psychologists, physicians, neurologists, or brain-mind researchers. You may not hold some of these premises; perhaps you may even hold some that contradict ours. It's not unusual in science, for example, for two psychologists to hold contradictory premises about human personality, and yet both be successful in treating people. Or, two physicists may hold contradictory assumptions about the structure of the physical universe, and yet both create valid mathematical equations to describe physical reality. So, it is not upsetting if in your own approach to dreams you hold different premises, nor if you disagree with one or more of our premises, even from the viewpoint of spirituality. If we listen to each other, we will undoubtedly learn from one another.

Here are our ten premises about dreams and spirituality.

*PREMISE 1.* THE DREAM IS, AMONG OTHER THINGS, A SPIRITUAL EVENT.

The dreamer of the mask dream recognized her dream as a spiritual event.

*The night after I had the golden mask dream I experienced a bright, golden light in my sleep. I woke up thinking someone had turned on the light in my apartment. I opened my eyes to find the room in total darkness, but when I closed them again I saw the incredibly bright light. So I opened my eyes again to check out my experience, and the room was still totally dark. I couldn't explain it. The inner light didn't go away for a long time—even after three or four times of opening and closing my eyes. I finally fell back to sleep. When I awoke in the morning, I connected the bright light experience with the melting down of the golden mask. [Melting the gold had been one of the alternatives suggested when the dreamer carried the mask symbol forward in time.]*

*Later that day, I sat in with the dreamwork group at the colloquium. There, a young man who was describing a dream about his spiritual center said, "it was hard and dark as coal." Spontaneously, I raised my hand and said, "But my center is liquid gold and sweet as honey." Intuitively, I sensed that the mask had melted and become liquid gold, and it was also a nourishing substance like honey.*

*The essence of my being was no longer a mask, my Self was no longer imprisoned by the mask. I realized instead that the symbol's energy could become a valuable resource for me, and I would eventually experience this transformation. It would happen.*

Dreams may be "the voice of the Self" or "the voice of the soul." They may also be, as many believe, "the voice of God." In any case, the dream always contains a spiritual component. As the dreamer of the child in the golden mask said,

*Doing dreamwork took me into the mystery of the incredible wisdom of the unconscious. It was awesome to see how perfectly the mask dream stated my situation in life. I felt blessed and guided by the dreamwork and the other dreams that came along to confirm the work I was doing. Each additional dream came just at the right moment and suggested the next step or addressed a missing piece of the process. How surely the voice of my soul spoke through my dreams and guided me each step of the way.*

*Working with the mask symbol brought me into a prayerful time. I prayed for strength and asked God for*

*help. I can look back at that dream now as a major break-through of the spirit and the beginning of my spiritual emergence.*

From earliest recorded history, people have observed their dreams and found in them a source of meaning, wisdom, and guidance for their lives. In fact, doing dreamwork has been an accepted spiritual practice for millennia.

Looking for meaning in dreams, a consistent spiritual practice in all major religions and most minor ones, is clearly acknowledged in the sacred writings of the Hebrews as well as those of the Christians and Muslims, the Hindus and Buddhists. Dreamwork is well-documented as a spiritual practice in just about every ancient religious tradition, including the Romans, Greeks, Egyptians, Syrians, Babylonians, Hittites, Canaanites, and others. Anthropologists report that dream-observing was and is practiced in East-Asian civilizations as well as in American Indian communities and in aboriginal and so-called primitive tribes on every continent. Wherever they found shamans, they found spiritual practices related to dreams.

According to our research, throughout the first five centuries of the nascent Christian church, believers often reflected on their dreams as a spiritual practice. By the fifth century, however, dreamwork began to be discouraged by the official hierarchy. It is very likely that one reason the fifth-century Christian church disapproved of its followers observing their dreams was because dream-watching was no longer carried on as a spiritual practice but had become a superstitious activity. People were no longer using dreamwork to develop their moral and spiritual growth, but rather were using it as a fortune-telling device to predict their future, increase their power over others, and further their material success. As one historian put it, "Many who followed their dreams were no longer interested in the God-life, but only in the good-life."

Even though dreamwork remained prohibited by the church for the next 1500 years, it continued to be practiced quietly throughout those centuries by holy men and women, many of whom became canonized saints. Now, in our own generation, dreamwork as a spiritual practice is again publicly blossoming.

The dreamer and the symbol work she did on the golden mask

dream put her into the ancient dreamwork tradition of interest in the God-life. She treated the dream and its symbols with reverence. To her, they were like a sacred gift. In response, she chose to develop the body, mind, and spirit God gave her, to be of service to her family and fellow humans, and to become as whole as she could be.

For example, when she carried the mask symbol forward in time, she said that she wanted to use the income from the sale of the mask to feed and nourish needy children. In waking life, she lived out that dreamwork choice by focusing on children and working as a clinical psychologist in a therapeutic nursery. She explained:

> *In Children's Services for the County, I worked as an advocate as well as a therapist. My first job was at a school for emotionally disturbed children. I freely gave many extra hours because it was something I really wanted to do. For example, I worked with Henry, who was essentially a little old man at age five and had never emotionally experienced childhood. Although I was scheduled to see Henry only once a week, I chose to see him every school day.*
>
> *Henry was like the child in the golden mask, except that he wore the mask of an adult. The feelings of the child behind the grown-up mask were underdeveloped. At age five, Henry had only one word for all feeling states—"funny." If a child on a bicycle ran into Henry or hit him, it made him feel "funny." If he felt a need to go to the toilet, it made him feel "funny." If he lost something, he felt "funny." Developmentally, when I first saw him, he was in a frozen state.*
>
> *But Henry's mask was not yet as rigid and set as mine had been. It hadn't had enough years to harden into metal. I was able to help him remove his "adult mask" before it became molded to him as an expected and accepted part of his character. The child part of Henry was undernourished. He desperately needed to experience being a child—to be encouraged to play and feel free to be messy. At home he had not been allowed to mess up anything. Without therapeutic intervention, Henry would have grown into adulthood as a powerfully angry child. With it, he was able to*

*claim his childhood and return to the regular classroom to socialize there and operate productively and happily.*

*PREMISE 2.* DREAMS ARE GIVEN FOR OUR HEALING AND WHOLENESS.

In part at least, the dream's purpose is to put us in touch with our ultimate values and get us involved in our own development and growth, especially our spirituality. The sequence of dreams following the mask dream led the dreamer deeper into an understanding of the ways she could help bring about the levels of healing within her that would take place during subsequent years. The mask dream had metaphorically stated the current imbalance in her personality and called her to wholeness.

In religious and spiritual traditions, the dream is viewed as a holistic event, that is, an experience of and for the whole person. In other words, the dream is given, not simply to the mind or the spirit, but for the benefit of the whole person: the living, interacting person. The dreamer was in need of wholeness, as she comments:

*At the time of the golden mask dream, I had been married for eighteen years. My life was quite comfortable by most standards. My husband had inherited wealth, liked to collect art, and generally indulged me. On the other hand, I had been careful to remain a good little girl: pretty, sweet, and nonthreatening; smart enough, but not too smart. I learned to echo my husband's views so naturally that I hardly noticed I didn't have opinions of my own, or even a sense of what I knew.*

*The mask dream spoke to my wholeness. It was the beautiful child and the angry child that I was being challenged to integrate and bring into balance, as well as the feminine mother and the masculine goldsmith who worked together to free the child.*

*The mask dream came to me at a time when I needed to develop my own wholeness in order to bring wholeness to others in my work. How could I teach others to love themselves and honor their rights if I was not doing it for myself? I chose to look at the truth of my own life in order to know both the struggle and the value in helping others search for their own truth.*

*I had the mask dream in the colloquium setting, where I was respected, valued, and affirmed as a person with an important contribution to make. It was an ideal, receptive time for me to receive the dream that would change my life.*

The child in the golden mask was not only undernourished, but was unable to hold its head up. Because of the mask, the child could hardly hear, be heard, see, breathe, interact with the world. The child in the mask was not fully alive. As the dreamer put it,

> *One of the clearest messages of the dream was that an entire dimension of myself, represented by the child in the mask, was not really alive in the world but was hidden away, constricted and unacknowledged. The dream was calling me to live life wholly.*

Looking at the dream as a holistic event places the dream into a larger context. From a contemporary scientific viewpoint, since the dream is a holistic event, it is thereby also a psychological event, a cultural event, a religious event, a neurological event, a mind-brain event, an event that is partly unconscious, an event that connects the unconscious (or deeper mind) and the waking ego. Because the dream is such a holistic event, it may be studied and researched legitimately by the psychologist, the anthropologist, the theologian, the philosopher, the physician, the neurologist, the consciousness researcher, the parapsychologist, and so on. Each discipline focuses on one or other aspects of the dream event. One discipline's focus does not deny the focus of another. By being open to many foci, one's own perceptions may be enriched.

Doing the different symbol techniques enriched the focus of the dreamer. In her own words:

> *When I carried the mask symbol forward in time (Technique 5) I gained a sense that to do what needed to be done, I would need to use my patience and my professional qualities. Taking off my mask might be hard work, but I*

would see that it was done skillfully—I would call in a professional to help me—so that the child in me would become fascinated with the process itself and lose some of its fear. And I would end up with a decision about what I wanted to do with the mask afterwards. I imagined that, as in the dream, it would be put into my hands. It would be up to me to see how and where the mask would be most useful in the larger community.

When I carried the symbol back in time (Technique 6), to see how the mask first came to be on the child, I realized that the lack of relationship with my mother arose, not out of my own unlovableness, but out of my mother's unconsciousness and inability to bond. It wasn't that the child had done something wrong.

The dream allowed me to begin to understand my mother and my relationship to her in a new way. Oddly enough, for the first time, after I worked on the mask symbol, our unfulfilling, painful, weird relationship began to make sense. I could look at my mother's neglect of me without all my usual anger or all my usual guilt (at not having been a "good enough" child). "If I had been more perfect," I used to think, "it would have made the difference." Now, I'm able to see my mother and her lack of awareness of my needs with some compassion and understanding.

In doing amplification (Technique 4), I discovered in making a list of the functions a mask can serve, how many different roles a person like me may be asked to play not only in the family, but in the larger community as well. All these roles somehow contributed to my being able to fulfill my unique purpose in life.

The mask dream had brought me to the place where I could begin to see my role in the world and the part that I could uniquely play in society.

## PREMISE 3. THE DREAM IS GIVEN IN SYMBOLIC LANGUAGE, THE LANGUAGE OF METAPHOR.

Although a dream sometimes portrays a believable story, it is seldom meant to be taken literally, since dream language is the symbolic language of myth, metaphor, and archetypal forms. Such language indicates that the dream is happening in *chairos* time, i.e., sacred time, the eternal now. The dreamer lies asleep at the intersection of *chairos* time and *chronos* time. As the clock ticks onward while the dreamer sleeps, the dream carries the dreamer into a sacred dimension, where a transfer of wisdom and energy occurs. What can only be accomplished with difficulty while the waking ego is in charge of consciousness can easily be done when the psyche steps into sacred time and is open to a dream. Later, using dreamwork, the waking ego draws out the dream symbols, as one might pull up buckets of water out of a well, and discovers them to be filled with archetypal gifts.

For people in spirituality who study dreams, the language of dreams is metaphorical. In order to learn the language of dreams you need to learn the language of metaphor. For this reason, finding meaning in a dream is not like translating a paragraph from German to English. It's more like turning a poem into prose, for example, turning the line of poetry "You are the sunshine of my life" into a paragraph of prose that spells out the physical, emotional, and spiritual meaning of that "sunshine" metaphor.

For the most part, metaphor is *the* language of spirituality. Metaphor is also the language of the spiritual domains of art, poetry, drama, story, and song, just as it is the language of meditation, creativity, courage, and dreams.

Some of the most powerful writings of all times are filled with metaphor. For example, here is how the ancient Hebrew prophet Isaiah described his call from God to prophecy to the people:

> Yahweh called me before I was born,
> from my mother's womb he pronounced my name.
> He made my mouth a sharp sword,
> and hid me in the shadow of his hand.
> He made me into a sharpened arrow,
> and concealed me in his quiver (Isaiah 49:1–2).

When the spirit speaks in a dream, it most often speaks in metaphor. The golden mask, a single image, pierced the dreamer's consciousness like a sharp sword. It enabled her to uncover and unravel parts of her life that were in need of development and to call her to live up to her highest capacities. It was as if, in the dream, God had said to her: "You now live encased in a golden mask. Will you choose life or death?"

*Recently, I've had the realization that the culture I live in has an ultimate value that my parents subscribed to: "Money is what gives you power and importance; it is the most important thing to possess, the one true measure of success." Even though people often say otherwise, as my parents did, their example belied their words. Acquisition of money was the most important thing to be about in the world. My parents "saved" money at any cost!*

*For me, the transformation of values, like the melting down of the mask's gold, had to do with the realization that money is important only in terms of the good I can do with it, not only for my own self but for others.*

*Having money doesn't guarantee security. What does is trusting either in my own ability to take care of myself or in being taken care of by those who love me, if I need it. This awareness enabled me to put aside having money as a major priority. The shift happened when I knew I was loved. I knew then that even if I were to lose all my savings, I'd be able to take care of myself, I mean, earn a living. And if I couldn't do that, there would be people who loved me enough to see that I was cared for.*

The dreamer did some dreamwork on the other symbols of her mask dream, finding it easier to explore them after doing extensive work on the mask, and discovered some of their metaphoric meaning for her.

*The good sweet little girl was really a metaphor about how I saw myself then and how the rest of the world seemed to see me. I also discovered that I valued—and hope I always will—being a good person, one who tries to live up to my best potential. I realized that being a good person is not the same as being a good little girl. For one thing, being a good person calls for inner direction and acting out of choice, not from fear of punishment.*

*The child in the mask after the mask was removed was not a pretty child. Its skin was dry, wrinkly, pale, flaky, and*

*irritated. Its hair was rubbed off and patchy. It found the
light of day startling. Its body was skinny and boney, not
plump like the good child's. I knew beforehand that when
I looked at it face-to-face I would feel guilt, shame, and
embarrassment, and I would have to deal with these emotions. At the same time I knew that I would need to nurture,
love, and heal this child, and take the time and effort required to help it become the beautiful child it could be.*

The goldsmith who symbolized the masculine qualities I would need to be able to remove my own mask, reminded me that I needed to be a professional in this pur-
suit, not just a dabbler.

In contrast, the can opener was a metaphor for crude
tools and techniques that I could misuse in the process. I
admit that I had been tempted to use sex, alcohol, and
drugs to break out of my mask. Other people I knew had
tried getting past their inhibitions or escaping their painful
imprisonment by going off on vacations and doing things
they wouldn't do at home, such as drinking too much, going to dangerous places, picking up sexual partners indis-
criminately. Others had tried to sidestep necessary psychological growth by buying a new wardrobe, moving their
homes, changing their jobs, marrying someone else. Such
tools would have been dangerous and inappropriate for me
not only because they really wouldn't work but also because they would cause more pain to me and others, and
especially because they would not have been in line with
being true to myself.

The Yellow Pages represented the rich resources available for finding what I needed. I was not alone. There was
an abundance of caring people, many options, and new
opportunities. I didn't have to settle for a can opener when
I truly needed a goldsmith. Help for me was not far away
and inaccessible, but near at hand and ready.

One important thing about the mother in the dream
was that she moved from being helplessly reactive in face
of the frightening situation of the child imprisoned in the
mask, to being creative in bringing about the result she
really wanted for herself and the child. Also, both the
child's and the mother's fears and anxieties were lessened

when they participated in the process of taking off the
mask. *My fear about the child being uncontrollable when
the goldsmith began his work didn't happen. Instead, the
two of us became fascinated by his work. The process of
taking off the mask got my ego involved and I could step
back and be an observer.* As long as I remained a conscious
observer, I didn't slip into my fears.

*PREMISE 4.* THE DREAM IS A GIFT, TO BE OPENED, USED,
AND CHERISHED. IT IS OFTEN ALSO A GIFT FOR THE
COMMUNITY.

In this dream-moment outside of *chronos* time, in this dip into
*chairos* time, we usually find a *gift* for our life, a source of energy,
an insight, a new alternative, the revelation of an unexpected potential. Dreamwork allows the dreamer to bring the gift of the dream—
wisdom, insight, energy—from sacred time into chronological
time. Thus, the sacred energies become accessible to the waking
ego. The various forms of spiritual practice, such as dreamwork and
meditation, are designed to help us find such gifts.

*One of the most important spiritual gifts I received when I
carried the mask symbol forward and did some dreamwork
on the new material was the discovery that I was already
lovable and loved. I no longer had to have as one of my
ultimate goals "to be lovable and loved." Now I could
focus my energies outward with a new goal of "being
loving."*

*Once at a workshop I accidentally bumped into one of
the participants and apologized for doing so. He turned to
me and asked if I was as gentle a person as I seemed.*

*At first, I said I didn't know. Then I was able to say,
"Yes, I am." I could own that I was the person he saw as
gentle.*

*But, even more dramatically, for one moment I caught
a glimpse of myself through the eyes of someone else, and
in that moment I realized clearly, "No wonder my children
love me! No wonder many of my clients love me! No
wonder many of my students love me!" In that special moment, I realized that I was indeed lovable and loved.*

*This reinforced the awareness that my ultimate value need no longer be "being loved" but could become "loving." To myself, my children, my clients, and my students, I could afford to be a truth-teller out of my loving, I could afford to be confrontational out of my loving. In my work and in my relating, I could become more fully-conscious rather than only self-conscious.*

*With this new awareness, I could do what I needed to do in relating to others, not as a reason for getting them to love me or to think of me as a nice person, but to do it out of my sense of loving.*

*I began to recognize the truth of the biblical call to love your neighbor as yourself—to recognize and participate in the fellowship of all people. I noticed, too, that "loving yourself" is equally a part of that biblical call. Therefore, to love and care for myself would be something good, desirable and appropriate.*

In almost all traditions, the purpose of bringing the discipline of spiritual practice into our lives is to be able to live our lives more fully and wholly, more in line with our destiny and life-purpose. In fact, we can't seem to live life fully and wholly unless we introduce some way of dipping into our deepest resources, unless we follow some spiritual practice.

*As I explored why it was important for me to deal with the mask symbol, I saw that its ramifications extended far beyond my own life and wholeness. The mask released the energy to want to make a difference in the larger world, to help others, to have an impact on the lives of the people I touched.*

*From the time of the mask dream, I began to keep a dream journal and make note of the things that were touching others. I remember recording a story of going with one of my daughters to a small jewelry shop. She wanted to exchange a watch given her by her father for something she liked better. The salesman proposed to give her a much less expensive watch (which she liked) as a trade. (He had*

*calculated it as though it were an even exchange.) I said,
"No. She also needs to receive the difference in value as a
cash refund." He said, "I am doing you a favor just to exchange the watch." I replied that there was no question of
a favor, but that my daughter had a right to exchange her
watch and have the difference back. My old way would
have been to say "Thank you" and politely leave, and not
point out that he was cheating us, which would have made
him angry and uncomfortable. Thanks to the energies from
my mask dream, I held my ground, and my daughter ended
up with the watch she preferred plus the difference.*

*I hadn't attacked the salesman or called him names. I
simply pointed out facts and our right to an exchange according to customary policy. I felt he certainly thought I
was a bitch, and I admit I wasn't very comfortable doing
the negotiations, but I did feel clear and strong about it,
and I walked out of the shop holding my head up.*

*As we left the store, my daughter said she was glad I
had been assertive. She said she wouldn't have known how
to do it herself, but now that she had seen me do it, she felt
she could do if she had to.*

Historically, as in the case of many biblical dreams, a dream was
viewed as given not only to the individual dreamer, but also to the
entire community to which the dreamer belonged. The mask dream
turned out to be a community dream.

For many days after the mask dream, other doctoral candidates
at the colloquium related to the original mask dream and became
conscious of parts of their lives that were hidden, unattended, undernourished. Moreover, in subsequent months and years, the same
mask dream has repeatedly had impact on those who heard the telling of it.

*At workshops, whenever I have told my mask dream, peo-
ple have personally thanked me for sharing the dream. Sub-
sequently, many have themselves begun working on a major dream in their lives. After hearing the mask dream, one
woman, I'll call her Marie, told me that she had a recurring*

dream of a child hiding fearfully in the back of an attic,
guarded by a big green monster. In the dream, the child
was cowering, frightened, starved like a "skinny refugee."
But Marie could not get to the child because the monster
prevented it.

Marie recognized the scared and hungry child as "the
feminine" part of herself that had been unattended and
undernourished since early childhood. Instead, for as long
as she could remember, she had preferred to emphasize
her masculine qualities, "trying to be the son that my father always wanted." Now, as an adult in her early forties,
she was about to leave a business career in a predominantly
male world and enter a women's religious community.

Marie's dream and my dream were both speaking to a
need for integration. Our opposites were lacking in us. She
needed to develop the feminine, I needed to develop the
masculine.

The influence of the mask dream was indirectly making other
people conscious of their holistic development and their need for
spiritual growth.

Looking back on it, I am thankful that I worked with the
mask dream because it called me to be a much more complex person than I had been. I broadened my focus from
working with learning-disabled children to serving people
of all ages. I began specializing in spiritual growth as well
as psychological growth, spiritual healing as well as psychological healing. I encourage my clients to pay attention
to their dreams and teach them to do their own dreamwork. Over the years, I have passed on the gift of dreamwork to many others.

## PREMISE 5. DREAMS AND DREAMWORK CAN BE USED TO RELEASE SPIRITUAL ENERGIES.

For Sigmund Freud, dreams were the royal road to the unconscious. For him, the unconscious realm was a boiling cauldron of
energy, and dreams led the way to this source of energy.

For Freud's disciple, Carl Jung, dreams brought archetypal symbols from the personal and collective unconscious into waking life. Some of the names he gave to these archetypes included *Masculine, Feminine, Hero, Adversary, Shadow, Persona, Death/Rebirth,* and so on. But what are these archetypes? For Jung, they were energy complexes: bundles of energy, like the myriad strands of electrical wire bundled together in a power cable carrying energy from one place to another.

One of the archetypes that revealed itself in the golden mask dream was the mask itself, the *persona.* In the Jungian system of consciousness the *persona* is a source of energy coming from the unconscious depths whose function is to provide life to our social and public faces. We all wear masks in our daily lives. Your personality (*persona* -lity) refers to the unique set of public faces with which you relate to people in your family and the larger community.

According to Carl Jung, "People who neglect the development of a *persona* tend to be gauche, to offend others, and to have difficulty in establishing themselves in the world."

Like everyone else, you probably have a dozen or more different masks, or public faces, that you put on and take off at will as you relate to different people—your parents, your children, students, shopkeepers, tradespeople, clergy, strangers, celebrities, old friends. Another way of getting in touch with your public faces, energized by the *persona,* is to list the different hats you wear, roles you play or functions you serve in your daily life. For example, at various times, formally or informally, you may play the role of a parent, a sibling, a child, a teacher, a friend, a shopper, a driver, an organizer, a dancer, a squash player, a computer operator, a student, a parishioner, a consultant, a gardener, a nurse. Or, more subtly, you may categorize some of the roles you play as: the good little girl or boy, the victim, the rescuer, the wimp, the intellectual, the competitor, the champion, the advice-giver, the complainer, the peacemaker, the vamp, the Romeo, the bitch, etc.

Each of these roles serves a well-known and clearly-recognized social function. The way you relate to your mother is different from the way you relate to your spouse, and both may be different from the way you relate to your children, or your students, or your customers or clients, or salespeople, or physicians. In each relationship, as you utilize the energies of the *persona* archetype, you put on a different face or wear a different hat. It would be very confusing to everyone if you related to your parents the same way you related to your spouse, or if you talked to a physician the same way you talked to your children, or if you revealed to the plumber who came to fix a faulty drain the same intimate secrets you might tell to your closest friend.

Some people mistakenly think that they must always be the same person—"I am just myself"—to whomever they are talking. This is not only psychologically impossible, but would be socially destructive. We all need masks to survive in society. The reason that nurses wear white uniforms and state troopers wear special hats and badges is because at a glance you know how to relate to them. For society to function efficiently you need to be able to distinguish shoppers from sales personnel, priests from parishioners, police officers from pedestrians, and firefighters from curious onlookers.

As one of the students in our dreamwork course commented, "I realized for the first time today that if the *persona* is recognized as a mask and accepted as a necessary part of us, it is perfectly okay and serves a vital purpose. I have struggled with the fact that not all the people in my life know who I really am. The hat I wear at work is much different from my school hat, or my home hat, and sometimes I feel as though I am presenting a false face to these people. I am now able to recognize and honor each different face I wear as valid."

But the *persona* is not just a closet full of hats. It is better viewed as an energy source, because it releases in you the ability to take certain actions in relating socially. Energy is the ability to do work. The woman who is a teacher does different work in the classroom than she does relating to her family at home or relating to the committee members of an organization to which she belongs.

The dreamer became aware of different *persona* energies that could be released by her mask dream:

> *The mask dream released a variety of energies in me:* the energy to be the child in the mask, *e.g., to express my anger and my wish for freedom from the unnatural restrictions and restraints caused by the mask;* the energy to stand up for my rights, *e.g., my right to have needs and to express them; to be respected, loved, and heard; not always to have to be sweet and beautiful;* the energy to deal with the mask itself, *e.g., to look at my wounded places and help them*

*heal, to ask for acceptance without having to wear the
"good girl" mask; the energy to hold my head up, e.g., to
respect my own authority and knowledge, to have a sense
of my own power and to take responsibility for it; the energy to hear and speak reality and truth, e.g., to evaluate
information and reality, to have opinions, to be a truth-
teller even if that might be unpopular, to choose life, face
it, and live it as consciously and as fully as possible.*

From the perspective of spirituality, the intent is that this archetypal energy be brought back into waking life and integrated into
our choices.

*PREMISE 6.* THE DREAM ALLOWS THE WAKING EGO TO
ESTABLISH RELATIONSHIP WITH OUR DEEPEST SELF.

*The mask dream wisely noted that I had not developed
certain hidden and forgotten parts of myself. In spite of the
sophisticated work I was doing with the learning disabled,
the dream revealed that I was very much still a child, under-
developed in certain ways, naive, superficial, not knowing
my own potential. For example, I was totally a "yes" girl to
my husband, I never expressed an opinion he didn't sanc-
tion, and I was used to being told by him how I should talk.
Moreover, he was fond of telling me how often I embarrassed him by what I did say in public.
   When I first had the mask dream, I was still caught up
in being the good little girl and worrying what the neighbors would say. I was unconscious of the forces of good
and evil in the world. In doing dreamwork on the mask
dream and other dreams, my waking ego began to unravel
those understandings and to see them and their implica-
tions in my life. I began to develop my own powers of
discrimination and evaluation, to discern what I believed.*

The following diagram is a simplistic sketch of the fundamental
paradigm of spiritual practice for those on the path to spiritual
growth.

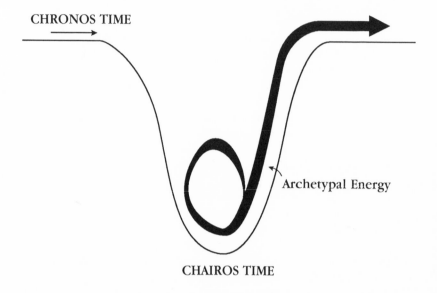

CHRONOS TIME

Archetypal Energy

CHAIROS TIME

The flat line stands for the chronological path of ordinary waking life. The arrows indicate the forward motion of life. The dip in the line stands for those moments, outside of ordinary waking life, when we get in touch with our spiritual resources. Usually, we get in touch by doing different spiritual practices, such as meditation, contemplation, centering, chanting, prayer, spiritual reading, looking at nature or beautiful pieces of art, listening to inspiring words or music, reflection, and of course through dreams and dreamwork.

When we do any spiritual practice, ideally speaking, we leave the ordinary waking world for a time and, in *chairos* time, dip into this archetypal-energy realm. *The reason we dip into this archetypal energy is to make available our deepest resources for personal renewal, direction, discernment, clarification, and so on.*

Like all night dreams, the golden mask dream happened in a non-ordinary state of consciousness. In this state, the dreamer's mind and spirit were open to the influences of the inner Self, the soul, and God.

As a bucket winds its way down into the deep well and serves as a container to bring a gift of water to the surface, so the dream and its symbols serve as containers that can hold and bring to the surface for you gifts of insight, inspiration, information, and energy that all come from your deepest sources of wisdom and guidance.

A dozen years later, according to the dreamer of the golden mask, those same dream symbols still contain the energies of transformation for her, and for all those who care to drink from those symbols.

It is important to underscore the assumption that the dream operates primarily, not in chronological time but in the sacred dimensions of *chairos* time. In chronological time, the dreamer did not give birth to twins, but in sacred time she did—and so do we all. In chronological time, the dreamer's child does not wear a golden mask that is both a constricting prison and a work of aesthetic beauty, but in sacred time her inner child does.

The purpose for tapping into the deepest energies of the self is *in order to bring those energies back and integrate them into our waking life.* So, from the standpoint of spiritual growth, the purpose of dreamwork, as with all spiritual practice, is to tap into our spiritual resources *in order to bring them into consciousness.* For the dreamer, her consciousness led her to act upon her awareness in specific choices.

> *Because of my mask dream and the symbol work, I made a choice to begin integrating the spiritual with the psychological in my life. For example, I took a position at Georgetown University in Campus Ministries, and I was willing to attempt to give a homily in chapel.*
>
> *Because of my dream and my growing interest in spirituality, I began looking for my own unique identity and purpose in the world and trusting that when an opportunity for spiritual growth was presented I would choose to take the chance, as when I was asked to give a homily or was invited to teach something on the common boundary between psychology and spirituality.*

From the spiritual director's perspective, dreamwork offers a way for developing and using a channel of communication between the waking ego and the deepest inner self. Jung would probably specify this deepest inner self as the archetype of the Self. For Jung, the Self is the center and integrator of all life experiences, conscious and unconscious. In religious language, it is the soul.

Establishing this ego-Self relationship is one of the most important spiritual tasks we do in bringing ourselves to spiritual maturity. The lack of it is probably the most common source of spiritual immaturity. Such a person we usually describe as "unconscious," referring primarily to a spiritual unconsciousness. On the one hand, psychological unconsciousness describes people out of touch with their feelings, memories, and psychological dynamics—most of which are usually evident to others. On the other hand, spiritual unconsciousness describes people out of touch with their inner resources and archetypal activity, unable to articulate their ultimate values, unconcerned with the meaning and purpose of their lives as well as their destiny; that is, the path, plan, and purpose to which we are called, or our reason for being in the world.

Notice that the ego-Self connection naturally fits into the fundamental paradigm of all spiritual practice. This paradigm presumes there is such a connection between the conscious and unconscious life; the ego-Self connection explicates it. It is very important to underline this principle again. Establishing this ego-Self relationship is perhaps one of the most important spiritual tasks we do in bringing ourselves to spiritual maturity.

Developing cooperation between the ego and the Self allows the ego to draw upon the deep wisdom of the Self and to bring more of what is unconscious into consciousness. In this connection, the ego gains access to a rich intuitive and creative layer of the psyche.

Developing an easy flow between ego and Self allowed the dreamer to make peaceful decisions and feel more clear about the path she was following. The Self could make a more effective input into the ego-perspective of things and help her to live more cosmically conscious.

*Dealing with death had always been a frightening thing for me. At conferences, I often found myself gravitating toward workshops on death and dying. At one of these conferences, I heard a presenter talk about life as a preparation for death. One prepares for this most important moment, he said, as a long-awaited, holy and deeply meaningful experience. Instead of fearing it, it became an experience for which you prepared.*

*Shortly after this conference, I visited a holy place in Medugorje, Yugoslavia. Resting on a tombstone in the*

*shady cemetery there, I realized that some years hence, for
certain, I'd be under a tombstone like this. And all the
worry I was currently expending on making money or being secure just didn't rank as important as what I was able
to do with my life. For the first time, I saw how meditating
or thinking about my death could be a very peace-bringing
experience.*

*In terms of my mask dream, even in the dream (before
the goldsmith came) I instinctively knew it was really important that the child in the mask know that it was accepted and loved before it died, if it had to die. It was not as
important to me, then, how long the child lived—though I
desperately wanted it to live—as it was that the child knew
it was loved. How long I lived was not as important to me as
how fully and consciously I lived.*

PREMISE 7. IN LIGHT OF SPIRITUAL GROWTH, THE
DREAM IS MORE POWERFUL WHEN LOOKED AT AS A
QUESTION RATHER THAN AS AN ANSWER.

When you do symbol work as a spiritual practice, it is much
better to look at the dream as a question rather than as an answer,
since the questions a dream tends to generate are related to ultimate
values and thus to spirituality.

One of the most basic dreamwork techniques we suggest in
*Dreams and Spiritual Growth* is called T.T.A.Q., which stands for
Title, Theme, Affect, and Question. We ask dreamers to give their
dream a title, to list its themes or issues, to identify the affect or
emotions that occurred to the dreamer during the dream. Finally,
we usually recommend that dreamers treat the dream as a question
and say: "If your dream posed a question about you and your life,
what would that question be?" When such a question is well-formu-
lated, it usually produces a burst of insight about the dream.

*The dream posed many questions to me about the child in
the golden mask. The first one that came to me was: Who is
this forgotten child? What part of me did this forgotten
child symbolize? Many other questions occurred as I
worked with the dream, such as: How could I have forgot-*

*ten the child? How did the child get into the mask? How was I going to get the mask off and let the child grow normally? What if the mask didn't come off? What then? But, supposing I got the mask off, how would I react to the child when I saw it? How would I integrate the child into my family? How would they welcome this child? (I knew they would rather not have to deal with it.)*

When she saw how the dream related to her present life, more questions tumbled out of her.

*The mask dream was also asking me: Do you want to nourish and develop the forgotten parts of yourself? Do you want to live fully and wholly? Do you want your wholeness more than you want the security that comes from being a good girl? Can you love the other parts of yourself that are not so sweet and pretty? Can you accept and love your whole self, including this other half of yourself? Do you have room in your life for this other child?*

These questions were really important to her and challenged her to clarify her ultimate values even more.

*One place I opted for wholeness came a few years after the mask dream, when I agreed to be director of the counseling center at Trinity College in Washington, D.C. To carry out my job there I had to rely not only on my therapeutic skills but also on the development of administrative skills. In order to deal with budget requests, create and defend programs that the students needed, and express my opinions effectively, I had to be assertive. I had to be confrontative as well as adaptable and flexible if I wanted to have a voice in helping shape school policy.*

A question invites relationship much more effectively than a command, especially the all-important ego-Self relationship. Questions also evoke more consciousness than answers. Whereas an answer often closes a transaction, a question keeps it open. Questions tap into symbol energy and keep it flowing.

## PREMISE 8. A DREAM IS INCOMPLETE WITHOUT DREAMWORK.

In spirituality, the dream is the gift; dreamwork is what we do with the gift. No gift is complete if you never open it and use it, but just leave it on the table in its original wrappings.

*My spirituality is an ongoing struggle between old and new values, past and present ways of being. I struggle with my old values of wanting to be safe and secure, make money, and be loved by everyone; and with the new values of wanting to be an instrument of love, healing, and consciousness in the world, a risk-taker, a truth-seeker, and a truth-teller. It is my choice in favor of these new values that has allowed me to stand up and speak publicly (whether teaching, preaching or lecturing) in spite of often almost incapacitating fear. In the minutes before any public appearance, my whole body usually becomes wet with the sweat of fear. I say things to myself like, "I'm going to be the center of attention, sticking my neck out. I've set myself up for evaluation and potential disapproval. If questioned, can I defend my opinion? What if I sound stupid? Or forget what I know? What if people don't like me?"*

*I've learned to ignore the fear as best I can, and it begins to go away as I focus my energy on what I want to give my audience and the result I want to create. In ordinary relationships, too, one side of me wants to be the good girl, quiet, agreeable, and not causing trouble; the other side may want to speak hard truths, assert my rights, say "no" or defend against abuse.*

*I struggle to discern what it means to be true to myself and my destiny. Who really knows their destiny? And yet, who doesn't feel called to live it as consciously as possible? I know that my childhood experiences are part of my destiny, since I believe that everything that has happened to me has meaning and a reason. For example, because of my childhood, I possess certain skills for listening, for knowing how to identify and tend to vulnerable places in others. My childhood caused me pain, but it also gifted me with compassion; it leads me today to think, write, and teach on*

*the importance of self-esteem; and it has led me to take up
a profession where my listening, compassion, and understanding can help heal others. And in the process, I can
experience my own value and healing.*

*I could have ignored the mask dream and stayed more
comfortable and secure, but I would have also foregone
the depth, the complexity, and the wonderful adventure of
my life. It makes me think of Joseph of Nazareth who in a
dream was told to marry Mary and be stepfather to the child
of the divine Spirit. He could have ignored his dream and
probably had a normal, comfortable, predictable life as a
carpenter in his hometown—with no need to escape a
murderous Herod by fleeing into Egypt. Joseph and I said
"yes" when invited by a dream into a larger destiny, and
we both have had to live with the consequences.*

*My personal spirituality includes finding models for
the energies I need, and St. Joseph has always been a special inspiration and comfort to me in my struggles with
fear. I'm sure there was good reason that the first words the
angel spoke to Joseph were, "Do not be afraid."*

*For me, to avoid fearful situations and to settle for
comfort instead of trying to develop and use my gifts in the
world would be to settle for being half alive. I might avoid
some of the pain, but I would also be avoiding some of
life's true richness and joy. Not to live my gifts is not to live
my life.*

PREMISE 9. DREAM TASKS ARE THE PRIMARY WAY WE
TAKE ACTION TO CHANNEL THE ENERGY AND INSIGHTS
OF THE DREAM INTO DAILY LIFE.

*The dream presents symbols of the kinds of energy available
to us in the unconscious and spiritual world.* Dreamwork allows
us to study a dream in light of the energies it can release. In practical
language, a dream can reveal to us when we are ready, i.e., when we
have the energy, to work on a certain psychological or spiritual
issue. After her dreamwork on the golden mask dream, she became
conscious that she must deal with evil in her life.

*I remember trying to come to grips with the problem of
evil. Before this time, I wanted to say that evil didn't really*

*exist, it was only a misunderstanding. But when I really
looked, I could see that some things were definitely destructive and harmful, so I wanted to have an understanding that would enable me to recognize what was evil and
what was not. I needed to learn to live in the world and face
the evil there, instead of trying to escape from it by wearing
a pretty mask.*

*As a child I used to hide in my closet with the door
closed, wrapped in a large, heavy comforter. And in different ways, I was still hiding in that tiny closet and keeping
the door closed to the rest of the world. Thanks to the mask
dream, I was choosing to come out into the light, leaving
the hiding place and the comforter behind. In the real
world, so new to me in a very real sense, I felt very vulnerable and exposed, and I didn't like those feelings. I still
don't. But I certainly preferred not to be hidden away alone
and constricted in darkness. I wanted to be able to take my
mask off and to give up having my security come first. I
certainly prefer to live in discomfort than to be hidden in a
closet—at least most of the time.*

Notice we didn't say the dream *tells* the dreamer to do something. Instead, it reveals when the dreamer is *ready and equipped
to do something.* (It sometimes also confirms when the dreamer is
already doing something.) Despite the conceptual clarity and emotional intensity of a certain dream and what it seems to mean, the
dreamer in waking life must still choose to respond to that dream.
The dreamer of the golden mask still had to exercise her waking ego,
the choicemaking part of her, in making a decision to take or not
take some approach suggested by the dream. The dream merely
establishes connection and communication between the dreamer's
conscious and unconscious life. But this is a very important
connection.

*The mask dream made a connection for me; namely, that I
had neglected developing my assertive masculine qualities, and that I needed to do so in order to balance my
receptive feminine ones. In the symbols of the two children, I could experience the polarity between their two
sets of qualities and I realized that what I had kept sepa-*

*rated in my life up to now needed to be integrated and harmonized.*

*At the same time as my outer marriage was coming apart, I was being called to an inner marriage of the masculine and feminine within myself.*

## DREAM TASKS

The final step in all dreamwork is to turn the energy and insight of the dream into choices and actions or a shift in perspective. At this stage, it is up to the waking ego, after reflecting on the energy and insight of the dream, to make choices for living, acting, relating, and thinking.

The easiest and most effective way of doing this is, as the golden mask dreamer did, to create a list of possible dream tasks that could be done to keep the energy of the dream alive, and to choose some of these dream tasks and actually carry them out.

Why actually carry them out? For two reasons. *First, if you don't use the energy released in the symbol it will slip right back into the unconscious and no longer be as readily available.* How many of us have had insights about our lives, important insights that we recognized as important, and we intended to do something about them, but we never turned those insights into do-able tasks. Consequently, our lives were never changed. Those great insights soon became just vague memories, taking up perhaps a line or two in our personal journal.

*The second reason we need to choose dream tasks and carry them out is that such tasks nurture the energy of the symbol.* The more we use a gift of energy, the more that energy becomes available to us. This principle is true in all domains of life: the more you exercise your muscles, the stronger they become and the more energy they make available to you. The more you discipline yourself to keep the symbol energy alive, the more access you have to it. If your dream reveals to you that you have the courage to face an important issue in your life, create a set of tasks to keep that energy alive, and exercise that courage energy. In doing so, you will develop courage to face not only that first issue but other issues that will come up in the future.

*I realized that to develop facility and courage in carrying out tasks I would probably need some help. By nature, I am* an extrovert and like to please people, but I find it difficult to ask others for anything. *(I am great at knowing or antici-pating what others might want, but often unclear about my own wants.)* One of my very early symbol work tasks was to identify areas for self-appreciation and self-development, and then to identify people whom I could ask to join me or assist me in these pursuits. Here are the seventeen catego-ries I started with:

1. Dreamwork
2. Gestalt work
3. Meditation practices
4. Poetry and creative writing
5. Journal-keeping
6. Spiritual reading and discussion
7. Play, i.e., silly fun
8. Theater and concert-going
9. Artwork and artistic expression
10. Movement and bodywork
11. Movies and dancing
12. Going on trips, picnics, and walks with children
13. Going on trips, picnics, and walks with adults
14. Finding comfort in times of distress (e.g., when I was sad, fearful, confused, etc.)
15. Good meals, nurturing, mothering (finding people who would invite me over for nourishment of body and spirit, provide me with a sense of being loved and cared about, of being special and important)
16. Intellectual conversation (to nourish my mind)
17. Decision-making (It has often been difficult for me to come to a decision; it usually feels like the world is full of either right or wrong choices, and I have been ill-prepared to evaluate realistically the options and the risks.)

Making the list was rather easy, fun, and stimulating. Taking the next step, to ask some of the designated people, took choice-energy and courage, sometimes a lot. I made it somewhat easier for myself by identifying two or more peo-

*ple for each category, and some names were listed in a
number of categories.*

*There were a number of people who were helpful to
me in developing the final category, but possibly the most
helpful was a woman who told me something that helped
me shift my perspective on decisions. She said, "There are
very few really right or wrong decisions in life, such as life
and death choices. Mostly there are just decisions to be
made, and some are more challenging than others to
live with."*

*Another friend took this piece of wisdom a step further
by pointing out that it was often through living with the
more challenging, less comfortable decisions that we grew
and developed the most.*

*The 14th category is probably the most dear to me,
because those who helped me with it were what I call
life-listeners and truth-tellers. These were the ones who
would listen to me talk about myself with genuine interest
and then with clarity and courage tell me the truth about
myself as they perceived it.*

We name three different kinds of dream tasks that you can use to
keep the energy of the dream alive.

The first are *Dreamwork Tasks*. These are additional dreamwork techniques that you can use to clarify and nurture the energy
revealed by the dream or by a symbol within the dream. Dreamwork
tasks that the golden mask dreamer did included doing symbol
work, having a dialogue with a dream figure, bringing a symbol
forward to resolution, doing artwork to concretize a dream symbol,
observing future dreams for confirmation, and so on. Such dreamwork tasks activated the energy of the dream symbol for her, even
though they did not directly bring it into her daily life. Dreamwork
tasks often lead into the other two kinds of dream tasks.

The second kind of dream tasks are *Personality Tasks*. These
are *inner activities* that you or your dreamwork partner or spiritual
director might suggest to keep the dream energy alive. Personality
tasks suggested to the dreamer of the mask dream were to: make a
list of the ways she was like or unlike the child in the mask, or jot
down what good things might happen to her if she were to realize a
certain symbol energy in her daily life, or begin the practice of some

personal discipline that would keep her connected with the symbol's energy, like marking down every time she asserted or affirmed herself. Other dreams and dream tasks may also give rise to personality tasks.

*I had a dream about being in a lions' den with seven hungry lions. (I had been reading the story about Daniel in the lions' den the day before.) I was terrified during the dream. It was really a nightmare.*

*I remember my dream partner asking, "How many lions were in the den?" I answered spontaneously, "Seven." When my partner then asked, "What were their names?" it surprised me, but I immediately began doing the task and naming the seven lions as Selfishness, Greed, Jealousy, Hypocrisy, Laziness, Fear, and Vanity—all aspects of me that I was afraid of. I recognized that each of them was dangerous to my Daniel part, the part that was striving for wholeness and holiness. I was also afraid other people would see those qualities in me and not love me. That's probably why the lions terrified me.*

*More importantly, they were parts of me I wanted to change and transform, so that their new names would be: Respecting My Own Needs, Generosity, Courage, Honesty, Creativity, Trust, and Self-Esteem.*

When asked what she learned about the lions dream and other personality tasks, she replied:

*I found especially helpful the dream task of naming the seven lions as seven fears I could own and treat as Shadow qualities. A Shadow quality, I had been told, was wonderful energy that needed to be named (identified), claimed (owned by me as a part of me), and tamed (transformed into productive, useful energy in the world, domesticated into a contribution to society). I tried to begin this with the new naming.*

*I also liked the dream task of dialoguing with many of my dream symbols and characters. I especially delighted in the image of a bitch puppy who had been living in a barn-*

*yard full of manure and only needed a bit of cleaning up. Part of a personality task, in dialogue with the puppy, had been to identify the manure, the various kinds of bullshit I had been living with. I needed to know what manure was embedded in my lifestyle, had clung to my self-image, or was stuck to my persona (the way I wanted to be seen by others). Whenever I got discouraged, I could dialogue with the frisky little bitch puppy, full of life and playfulness who was willing to trust and love, that I knew my daughters and I needed in our house.*

The third set of dream tasks are *Outer Life Tasks*. These are *outer activities* that you or your dreamwork partner might suggest to keep the dream energy alive. Outer Life Tasks might include taking actions that involve other people or the work you do. If your dream revealed that you, like the golden mask dreamer, had the energy to build your courage, you might choose to practice simple acts of assertiveness, or stand up for yourself among your friends, or to write a letter of complaint to some company. Even apparently less-helpful Outer Life Tasks may provided a dreamer with important insights.

*One task suggested to me related to nurturing was to learn to cook gourmet meals and enjoy cooking as a form of meditation, as one of my friends did. After inviting a few friends over for a gourmet meal, I made a special effort at cooking, taking several days to prepare for this event as an expression of my caring energy. The dinner went well, but being so focused and concerned about the food was not really an important value to me. It was much more important to be focused on my friends. After my second try at being a gourmet cook, I decided it just wasn't me, and I went back to my usual style of entertaining: having pot luck, pot roast, deli or, my favorite, Chinese carry-out to eat, and to focus my energy on bringing people together for a purpose and facilitating their interaction. In doing this task, however, I learned it was probably very important for me to find out* who or what I was not (I was not a gourmet cook) as who I was (a facilitator).

When asked what she had learned after doing a variety of tasks, the dreamer replied:

*The personality tasks and outer life tasks that dreamwork partners suggested helped me to translate some of my new ultimate values into everyday behavior. As a result, I was no longer so sweet and goody, but began to be a bit "pushy" and occasionally even argumentative.*

*I wasn't able to be assertive on my own behalf at first, but someone had asked if I could be assertive for the rights of my children, my clients, and my friends. I said yes. I began by being assertive for those others, and eventually I was able to be more assertive for myself.*

*For example, I had contracted with a landscaping service to do a job in our backyard. Not only did they plant the trees in the wrong places, but they had not completed what they promised to do. I complained and withheld payment. That was a big step for me.*

*When I thought people were not giving me good service or not caring for my health and welfare, I began to complain. Some of my rather clumsy first attempts resulted in changing my doctor, dentist, and lawyer.*

*I noticed one of my friends, Rita, seemed to be very assertive and made lots of requests. I admired her a lot, I realized, and so I asked her how she had learned to be so comfortable asking people for what she wanted. She said she didn't used to be that way. For years, she had asked for very little and had gotten very little. She noticed she wasn't getting much, so she decided to push herself to ask for a lot more, and ask more frequently. In her new strategy, she didn't get everything she asked for but she was getting a lot more than she used to.*

*One of the things I especially liked about Rita was that she was direct. You generally knew what she wanted and where you stood with her. She could be counted on to ask for what she wanted, and you didn't have to guess. I also noticed she didn't get upset or hurt when refused, she didn't even seem discouraged. (I had always thought that a refusal meant I should not have asked, that my asking had been inappropriate, insensitive or downright wrong.) Rita said she figured if she wasn't being refused sometimes, she probably wasn't asking for enough. I had a long way to go to be like Rita and I may never get there, but at least I have a model.*

The objective with dream tasks is to choose tasks that will keep the energy alive, not exhaust it. Therefore, choose tasks that are do-able in a finite amount of time, and tasks at which you are likely to succeed. Success breeds success. And a successful expression of dream energy is most likely to keep that energy alive. Better to have a string of little symbol work successes than one grand failure.

In assigning dream tasks, follow the example of the wise piano teacher. She will introduce you to the skill of playing the piano with a series of simple exercises at which you are most likely to succeed. When you have succeeded with each of these simple tasks, she will invite you to move up to the next level. And when you have succeeded at that level, she will invite you to move to a higher level, and so on. Eventually, you will have access to a full range of piano-playing energy. But it may take years.

So it is in spirituality, you move step by step through each level of spiritual growth until you have access to a full range of spiritual energies. It will take years. In that process, working with dreams and symbols can be very helpful.

PREMISE 10. THE PURPOSE OF DREAMS AND DREAMWORK IS TO BRING US TO CONSCIOUSNESS, THAT IS, TO AWARENESS PLUS APPROPRIATE ACTION.

In the Judeo-Christian tradition, the purpose of human life is to achieve salvation. But part of the meaning of that word "salvation" has to do with health, healing, and wholeness, which is meant to happen during this life, not just in heaven. Thus, it has always been part of the ultimate values of Western civilization to work for a better world, to bring about a lasting peace in freedom and equality for all. Other religious traditions may believe that all material reality is no more than illusion, therefore there is no reason to work for a better world; it is enough to relieve some sorrow and suffering along the way. Nevertheless, most of us feel called at the deepest level to translate our insights into action, and that action usually means to build a better community and environment for ourselves and those we care about.

Some approaches to dreams are content with helping the dreamer find meaning in the dream. Once they have found out what the dream is all about, the problem is solved and the process is over. Perhaps in certain approaches to the dream, it is enough to stop there. But in spirituality, which has to do with the way you think and act in the world in light of your ultimate values, the purpose of the dream and dreamwork is always consciousness.

Consciousness is a very "in" term these days, but not everyone has a clear definition of what it means. Many people equate consciousness with *awareness*. For them, coming to consciousness would be the same as becoming aware of something; they see it as an intellectual event, nothing more. But, as we said earlier, consciousness means more than just awareness. It is a holistic experience, not just an intellectual one. For us, *consciousness is awareness PLUS appropriate action*. According to this definition, an insight never becomes truly conscious until you put it into action, somehow, in your daily life, so that the insight changes or enhances you in some way.

*The mask dream never told me that bringing insights into everyday life would be easy. A few years after the dream, I was invited to teach some graduate courses as an adjunct faculty member. For me, graduate teaching brought with it a new sense of authority and an implication that I had opinions and thoughts worth stating. By accepting the job, I was asking to be heard and seen as a skilled professional, like the goldsmith. At first, I was quite uncomfortable, but as I continued to do it, I felt freer and more empowered and I finally grew to love teaching as an opportunity to evoke consciousness. Especially, I am pleased to notice that as a graduate-school teacher I have also been nuturing and attentive to my students, so I am still using my feminine qualities of openness, relating, and affirming.*

*Very early in my teaching I had an enormous aware-
ness. I realized much of my terror was that I didn't see my
students as separate individuals; instead they were all my
critical mother ready to dissect and reject my every state-
ment. No wonder I was frightened, surrounded by twenty
or more embodiments of my mother! To shift my percep-
tion, I had to consciously see each person as unique, and to
tell myself over and over that they were here because they
wanted to learn from me, that we were all on the same side,
and interacting in an accepting and friendly environment. I
had to work at integrating my new insight, so learning the
name of and something about each person became one of
my first tasks with every new class.*

To say that the purpose of spiritual practices, like meditation or
dreamwork, is to tap into inner resources in order to make them
conscious, means they need to be brought back and integrated into
our ordinary life choices. *Spiritual practice is always a matter of
consciousness,* and a spiritual practice is never complete until the
energies it is releasing are being incarnated in your life. Spirituality
always involves values and choices being made in everyday life.

*Because of my work with the symbols in the mask dream, I
began listening to Bible stories as if they were dreams of
mine. I felt the symbols in them would bring me new wisdom, if I allowed them to speak to me in my life as the
dream did.*

*I recall hearing the story of Jesus meeting the Samari-
tan woman at the well (John 4:1–42), and I found myself
listening in a new way. She became a powerful symbol for
me. I watched her behavior and the way she related to
Jesus. She was very direct with him and didn't hesitate to
ask him questions. Although she was probably somewhat of
a disgrace to her community, she wasn't embarrassed that
Jesus knew about her many husbands. Rather, she was
awestruck by it and considered Jesus a prophet. From this,
she launched into a number of questions about life, truth,
worship of God. By talking to him, she was breaking religious customs of her day, since Jews and Samaritans did*

*not talk to one another. She certainly didn't stay in the
socially accepted female role of that time.*

    *Like the Samaritan woman, I have found myself break-
ing the traditions of women as defined by my family. I also
broke a religious custom in our church as a woman by
giving a homily. I have begun to confront and ask more
questions of the authorities in my life.*

    *Perhaps more importantly, I find myself teaching and
doing therapy out of my own experience, just as the
woman at the well taught the people of her town about
Jesus out of her own experience. Sharing my golden mask
dream with classes and workshop participants has been a
good example of this.*

    *I discovered that the women students in my classes
often use me as a role model. "It's not so much what you
say as who you are and the way you are," was the way one
student put it. Another said to me, "If you can do it, so can
I." She felt she could do whatever she needed to do in
order to honor the value of her own life.*

Meditative and contemplative experiences are also often highly
symbolic and, in order to be understood, may need to be processed
by techniques akin to symbol work.

    *After meditating on the Samaritan woman at the well, I
realized she was a model for me. She symbolized a woman
who was sure of herself. She asked the questions that were
on her mind and wasn't easily intimidated. She listened,
learned, reflected, and challenged. She drew conclusions
from what Jesus said and checked out her ideas with him.
She could recognize another person's greatness and wasn't
embarrassed about her past. She wanted to share with her
community what she had learned and offer them the same
opportunity for growth she had enjoyed. She knew how to
get people to listen to her and stimulate their interest.*

    *I realized she could be symbolic of the strong woman I
wanted to be. She could do what Jesus' disciples apparently dared not do, that is, to ask Jesus hard questions about
who he was and what he was doing and saying. She acted as*

*an "equal," that is, she didn't feel intimidated, anxious or
hesitant.*

*I especially liked how she honored her curiosity.
That's a quality I know I have, but too often I feel intimidated and don't dare to ask the questions I have, or I feel
it's not polite to ask.*

In the spiritual life, the dream does not make the decisions or
choices for you. Most dreams and symbols simply metaphorically
reveal or reflect what is going on in your life and possibly put your
current situation in a fresh light, a light from which you can see your
experience from a new perspective and grow holistically. No matter
how clear a symbol or dream may be, your waking ego must still
become conscious, and it demonstrates that consciousness by making choices using the data revealed by the dream and your dreamwork. With dreams and dreamwork as a spiritual practice, there is no
substitute for self-reflection and choicemaking. The dreamer recognized that the choices facing her were up to her. No one else would,
or could, make them for her.

*I remember about this time that I felt I needed to be in-
volved in the larger community of humankind, for example, to be concerned about the survival of the human race.*

*My daughter Evie was about sixteen. One day she said
to me in a kind of offhand way that, because of the prolifer-
ation of nuclear weapons, she wasn't expecting to have the
opportunity to grow old.*

*I was shocked. Her words were heartbreaking. There
was my beloved child. My life's focus had been on developing my children to be the fullest and best persons they
could be and bring the gift of themselves to the world. If
the world might not survive and Evie might not be allowed
to live out her potential and make her contribution, what
did life mean?*

*I said to Evie, "How can I make sense out of my life if
you might never have a chance to grow and develop?"*

*She replied, "If there's anything you think you can do
that will make a difference, do it now, mom. Don't wait."*

*Because of her request, I decided to continue teaching
and writing, despite all my feelings of inadequacy and inse-*

*curity in these fields. I continued because I felt in that work I might make a difference. I figured I had to try to do whatever I could do. So, I rechose teaching and writing over and over, in spite of fear and poor self-esteem.*

*This book, too, is part of that effort. I must admit I feel painfully exposed by the information contained in it. I only hope by risking this exposure I may help others to begin building consciousness and self-reflection in their own lives. I want to encourage caring relationships and harmony, to feed the hungry both within and without.*

## CONCLUSION

From the perspective of spirituality and spiritual practice, symbol work and dreamwork are designed to promote consciousness and personal growth, and to release in people the energy to transform their lives in healthy and healing ways.

Dreamwork, rediscovered in the early 1970s as an ancient Judeo-Christian spiritual practice, has made one of the most revolutionary contributions to spirituality in centuries. Dreamwork—and symbol work as part of it—is really a spiritual practice that almost everyone can learn with some degree of proficiency and use effectively without having to be dependent upon some expert. It is a versatile and adaptable activity that can be used individually, but also with partners and in small dreamwork groups.

Since you dream every night, there is never a dearth of symbol material for spiritual growth. It is always there for you to tap into if you choose to, whenever you choose. There is no need to become enslaved to dreamwork. Seek its wisdom whenever you feel the need, for example, when making decisions or transitions, not because you should but because you can. Whether you choose to do dreamwork seldom or often, your dream source, your deepest inner self that loves you more than any mother ever could, will never cease to call you to your true greatness through your dreams.

*Part III*

# The Symbol Techniques

# AWARENESS TECHNIQUES

## SYMBOL TECHNIQUE 1

### Identify Symbols in a Dream Report

If you would like to reflect on powerful symbols from a certain dream, it is best to begin by writing out the dream in detail—all those details you can remember. The dream report is the foundation of all dream work, because it is the record of your original dream. It provides a source to which you can always refer.

OBJECTIVE:

■ to write down the details of your dream so that you can identify the various symbols in the dream.

*The Question to which This Technique Responds:*

What are the major symbols in this dream?

STEPS:

1. Write down the dream in all its details as completely as you can recall it. (If you have already written a dream report, skip to Step 4.)
2. As you write, be very specific in describing each character, figure, object, and event.
3. Include from the dream the feelings and emotions that were associated with each symbol or event. (If you are not aware of the different feelings you had during the dream, take a moment, as

you write your dream report, to re-create the dream scene and become aware, in retrospect, of how you felt or might have felt during each scene in the dream.)
4. After you have finished writing the report, reread it. As you do, *underline those symbols (persons, places, things, words, sounds, feelings, etc.)* that were important to you, e.g., that struck you as odd, powerful, unusual or that evoked strong emotional response in you.

## COMMENT

A very simple technique, this is the best preparation for helping you choose the symbol on which to do symbol work (Symbol Technique 2). Doing it may take up to fifteen minutes, resulting in a page or more of dream report with a number of symbols underlined.

In the dream of the child in the golden mask, the dreamer had underlined a number of symbols including the sleeping child, the crying child, the can opener, the telephone's Yellow Pages, the goldsmith, as well as the golden mask itself.

# SYMBOL TECHNIQUE 2

## Choose a Symbol on Which to Focus

Doing symbol techniques presumes you have already done some basic work on the dream, such as writing a dream report and noting some of the issues, themes, and feelings produced by the dream.

OBJECTIVES:

- to sort out which symbols in the dream generate the most interest and emotional intensity for you.
- to select a sequence of symbols for symbol work.

*The Question to which This Technique Responds:*

What symbol do I want to work on at this time?

STEPS:

1. On a sheet of paper, make a list of all the symbols you underlined in your dream report.
2. Next to each symbol, indicate whether you were attracted to the symbol (←), repulsed by it (→), both attracted and repulsed (← →), or felt neutral toward it (0).
3. Mark with an asterisk those symbols that produced the most powerful effect in you.
4. Rank the symbols in the sequence you would like to work on them.
5. Focus on the symbol ranked first and do a number of techniques based on it. Keep a record of the symbol work you do.

COMMENT

This technique takes only a few minutes, but can quickly clarify which symbol is most appropriate for you to work on now. Normally, in a dream there are some symbols to which you are attracted, others which evoke a negative response, and still others which produce little or no effect in you.

For the dreamer of the golden mask dream, three characters—the child in the mask, the sweet sleeping baby girl, and the goldsmith—had attraction energy, the can opener had repulsion energy, the crib and the Yellow Pages evoked little or no energy, while she found the crying child and the mask itself both attracted and repulsed her.

You may choose to work first on a less major symbol. For example, if you dream of your recently deceased grandmother handing you a glass of water, the grandmother may be a more important symbol, yet you may choose to work first on the glass-of-water symbol. The crying child in the mask was certainly a powerful symbol, yet the dreamer chose to work first on the golden mask itself. She would, of course, work on the child as a symbol later on, but she chose to do extended work on the mask to begin the process.

# SYMBOL TECHNIQUE 3

## Get Immersed in the Symbol

This immersion technique is essential if you are working with a dreamwork partner, counselor, therapist, or in a dream group. Immersion is one of the best ways to get both dreamer and dreamwork partners fully involved with the chosen symbol, because it brings about heightened awareness of the symbol. It presumes you have chosen a symbol on which to work.

OBJECTIVE:

- to guarantee that the symbol in the partner's mind and imagination is similar in its details to that which is in the dreamer's mind and imagination.
- to heighten the dreamer's awareness of the symbol, clarify its details, develop a relationship with the symbol, and produce metaphoric statements and insights into the symbol's meaning and energy.

*Question to which This Technique Responds:*

What is the symbol in all its details as it is experienced by the dreamer?

STEPS:

1. Re-create the dream scene in your imagination and experience the symbol in all its details. (Immerse yourself in the symbol.)
2. Invite your dream partners (or therapist or counselor) to ask you objectifying questions about details of the symbol. (N.B. Objectifying questions are not those about the symbolic meaning or interpretation of the symbol, but only about its sensory and emotional details. Objectifying questions usually begin: How much? How far? How big? How loud? How thick or thin? What color? What shape? What location? etc., etc.)
3. Partners continue asking objectifying questions until everyone

sees in their own imagination the symbol in much greater detail than before.
4. As dreamer, note what insights occur about the symbol and yourself as a result of this technique.

## COMMENT

Without doing this technique, you and your partners may be exploring different symbols. For example, when you first read the dream of the golden mask, you may have pictured spontaneously a mask that looked like someone you knew, some artistic sculpture, an African ritual mask or a medieval death mask. Only by asking immersion questions of the dreamer could you correct your perceptions.

This symbol technique proved very revealing for the dreamer, for, as she reported:

> *As I was doing the technique, I got in touch with feelings of entrapment and constriction I have known personally, and still know. As I answered their questions, I heard myself responding metaphorically about myself—not being able to hold my head up, seeing a distorted reflection of myself, having my vision and hearing obstructed, feeling my brain crushed, and dying inside the mask. In doing this technique, I could already feel welling up inside me the energy to begin removing my mask and reclaiming the parts of me that had been hidden and forgotten.*

SYMBOL TECHNIQUE 4

Amplify the Symbol

Amplification is an enjoyable clarifying technique, especially when working with a partner or in a group. When doing symbol work with a partner or others, be sure to do symbol immersion (Symbol Technique #3) before you do symbol amplification.

OBJECTIVES:

- to compile a list of the possible issues and emotions the symbol may be addressing, symbolically and metaphorically, in your life.
- to begin sorting out those issues and emotions that the symbol actually evokes.
- to put aside those that it doesn't.

*Question to which This Technique Responds:*

What functions does this symbol serve in ordinary life?

STEPS:

1. On a sheet of paper, list the many different functions this symbol can have in ordinary life. List them as action verbs whenever you can. Thus, some of the functions of the mask were: to hide, to distract, to entertain.
2. If you are working with a partner or group, invite everyone to add to the list to help amplify the function of the symbol.
3. When a possible function has been stated and listed, you the dreamer should say whether or not it is a "hit," that is, whether you have a felt sense that this function applies to the symbol in your dream. In other words, does it ring true for you or not? You will intuitively perceive some functions as hits and others as not.
4. Specially mark each hit function. Those marked as hits are functions to explore; they may point to certain ways of thinking and acting that you may want to question.
5. Note what you learned about the symbol and yourself from doing this technique.

COMMENT

Symbol amplification is especially useful as a basic technique for working with recurring symbols.

For example, recently the golden mask dreamer had a series of dreams, all within a month, in each of which at least one or two people had cancer or were dying of cancer. In different dreams, the cancer took different forms such as leukemia, lung cancer, or brain tumors. But the common symbol in all these dreams which called for study was "cancer." Here, symbol immersion (Technique 3) would be of little help, since immersion requires a specific, individuated, concrete symbol, while cancer is a generic symbol. In contrast, amplification allowed her to work with a non-individuated symbol, that is, a symbol that takes many forms.

Here are some functions of cancer that did *not* ring true for her as hits: cancer generates fear, provides a way to die, debilitates you, causes people to avoid you, sets you apart, gives you permission to take pity on yourself, evokes sympathy from others, gets others not to make demands on you, eats you up alive, forces you to undergo painful treatments.

In contrast, the following functions were all hits for her: cancer gives you permission to take care of yourself, allows you to change the way you live, causes you to change the way you look at life, calls you to make some important life choices, makes you think about how you will spend the rest of your life, gives permission to do things such as taking trips, resting, focusing on your health without feeling guilty.

The dreamer commented:

> *The issues in my life that I'm struggling with now include: trying to make some major choices about the use of my time and my life, trying to justify taking vacations and being away from my patients, and trying to look at what is the best use of my time in light of the contribution I want to make to society. Presently, I struggle with feeling guilty whenever I take time for myself. Yet I know that I feel called to set aside time to do some serious writing as well as some playing, resting, and just being.*

Carry the Symbol Forward in Time

This technique is to be used after the previous two techniques, especially if at the end of the dream the symbol's role in the dream (or event) remains unclear or unresolved, for example, when the energy of the symbol is not quite revealed in amplification.

Carrying the symbol forward is done by reentering the dream imagery meditatively in a waking state.

OBJECTIVES:

- to reveal more clearly to you the function and meaning of the symbol
- to generate more information about the symbol and possibly a sense of resolution, by finding out what happens to the symbol in the future.

*Questions to which This Technique Responds:*

What happens to the symbol when you carry it into the future? Where does the symbol go from here?

STEPS:

1. Take a few moments with eyes closed to relax.
2. In your mind and imagination, re-create the scene in the dream where the symbol last occurred. Re-create the emotional context of the symbol too.
3. When the symbol has become clear to you, allow yourself to watch the symbol as your imagination moves it forward in time. (Some symbols, like the golden mask, evolve and transform quickly, in a few minutes or an hour of dream time; other symbols may have to be carried forward for months and years, or even centuries, of dream time. The passage of dream time, of course, takes place in your imagination and may consume only a few minutes of clock time.) It is much like stopping a film in the middle of the story, and then starting it up again but focusing

only on one aspect. (You may recall a French film called *The Red Balloon* in which the viewers followed only the actions of the red balloon.)

4. If you are doing dreamwork with a partner or counselor, you may describe aloud to them what is happening to the symbol as it evolves in your imagination.

5. Continue carrying the symbol forward until it changes enough to give you more information or possibly to provide a sense of resolution.

6. Return to your ordinary consciousness and note what you learned about the symbol and yourself from this process. (You may also wish to treat this process as a dream and write a dream report on it.)

## COMMENT

When the dreamer used this technique on her golden mask, it provided a wealth of new insight and comfort for her (see pages 24–27). It also brought a sense of resolution because the mask was finally removed and the child was clearly safe. As a result of carrying the symbol forward, she could now deal separately with two major symbols: the child and the golden mask. Before doing this technique the child and the mask had been inseparable.

Carry the Symbol Backward in Time

This technique will provide best results when used after immersion and amplification, especially if the initial appearance of the
symbol or its origins is unclear, unexpected or unresolved. For example, in the golden mask dream, how the mask got to cover the
baby's head was unclear and its presence unexpected.

This technique, like Technique 5, is carried out by reentering
the dream imagery in a meditative state.

OBJECTIVES:

■ to uncover additional information about the symbol.
■ to bring about insight by finding out the origins or history of the
symbol.
■ to discover the roots of the symbol in your life.

*Questions to which This Technique Responds:*

How did this symbol evolve to its present context? What are the
origins of this symbol? How did it arise?

STEPS:

1. Take a few moments with eyes closed to re-create in your mind,
imagination, and feelings the scene in the dream where the symbol first occurred.
2. When the symbol has become clear, allow yourself to watch the
symbol as your imagination moves backward in time. It's like
starting with the sequel, then going back to read the author's first
book; or like seeing *Rocky II* or *III,* focusing on the relationship
with his wife, then going back to *Rocky I* to see how they first
met. (Some symbols reveal their origins quickly, in a single
scene or two; other symbols may have to be carried backward for
months, years or even centuries of dream time. This process, of
course, takes only a few moments in ordinary waking time.)
3. If you are doing this technique with a partner or counselor, you

may describe aloud to them the events happening in your imagination as you regress through time.

4. Continue carrying the symbol back in time until it changes enough to give you more information or insight about its origins. You may stop when you reach some sense of resolution.

5. Return to your ordinary consciousness and note what you learned about the symbol and yourself from this process.

## COMMENT

In carrying the golden mask back in time, the dreamer was able to discern that her mother played an important role in creating the mask. The scene generated by the technique implied that in subsequent therapeutic work, issues with her mother would be important to identify and work through.

## Associate to the Symbol

Though this simple yet powerful technique may be used at any time, it produces the most useful insights after doing some of the earlier symbol techniques (3, 4, 5, and 6).

Symbol association is usually led by a partner or counselor, though it can be carried out alone by the dreamer.

OBJECTIVES:

- to clarify the key issues related to the symbol that are active in your life today.
- sometimes, to reveal the roots of certain issues in your life.
- to link the dream symbol to other powerful symbols in your life (usually to symbols and events that reflect the issues brought up in the dream).

*Questions to which This Technique Responds:*

And what does *that* symbol remind you of? What are some other symbols from your daily life that connect with this dream symbol?

STEPS:

1. Your partner begins by asking you: "What does symbol X remind you of?" (Instead of saying "symbol X," the partner names the symbol itself, e.g., "What does the golden mask remind you of?")
2. You name the object, event, or person the symbol reminds you of, e.g., "A Henry Moore sculpture."
3. Your partner then asks you: "And what does a Henry Moore sculpture remind you of?"
4. You name the person, place, or thing a Henry Moore sculpture reminds you of, e.g., "A sculpture I have in my garden."
5. Your partner then asks you: "And what does the sculpture you have in your garden remind you of?"
6. Continue the question-and-answer process until you find your-

self responding with the image of a person, place, or thing that brings insight, i.e., a hit. "It reminds me of myself as a deprived child, begging for love and attention, begging not to be hurt."
7. Once a hit occurs, i.e., an inner "click" for you as dreamer, you may stop the association process, and note what you learned from this technique about the symbol and yourself.

## COMMENT

As a partner, it is important to know when to stop the process: when the dreamer reports a hit, i.e., a meaningful connection. Often you may recognize the look of a hit on the dreamer's face; but, to be sure, ask the dreamer if a hit has occurred.

The process works best when you, the partner, encourage the dreamer to respond to your questions with images and pictures rather than with abstract thinking or the description of feelings. If the dreamer is tending to respond abstractly, phrase your questions to evoke images. For example, if the dreamer says, "It makes me think of truth," reply by asking, "When you think of the abstract idea of 'truth' what picture or image comes into your mind?"

Sometimes the dreamer has more than one immediate association to the symbol, in which case choose one association and follow its lead until a hit occurs. Then, if the dreamer wishes, take the second association and follow along the path it takes you until a hit occurs.

As you work more and more with dream symbols, you also begin to look for the symbolic and metaphoric events in your daily life experiences. For example, the dreamer of the mask dream reported that one morning she was walking along an ocean beach in New Jersey when she discovered some money and a man's billfold on the sand in front of her. In a reflective mood, she decided to make some symbolic associations. "What does finding someone's billfold on the sand remind me of?" she asked herself.

"Of being entrusted with other people's lives," was what first came to mind. That was a hit, for indeed she saw her life and her work, both teaching and therapy, as being entrusted with other people's lives.

Then another association occurred to her: "Of having a sense of stewardship about possessions." That too was a hit, since she had been struggling with how to invest her money at the time, and although much of her money was earned, some of it she had just stumbled across, so to speak, like the money in this wallet. Although she planned to find the owner of the wallet and return everything to him, she wondered what her responsibility was in managing the money that had been entrusted to her, i.e. in her own billfold.

A third association occurred to her: "The sacredness of having something that someone else needs, whether it be their billfold, some money, wisdom, understanding, support, or insight." For her, the billfold also symbolized all the patients and students that find their way to her by accident in search of learning, healing, wholeness, or something else that they need. "I wanted always to remember the sacredness of that stewardship."

## SYMBOL TECHNIQUE 8

### Name Some Energies Released by the Symbol

Whenever dreamwork is related to spiritual growth, identifying the energies, insights, and other gifts given by the symbol is a primary step in the process of coming to consciousness (i.e., awareness plus appropriate action). This technique is the culmination of the previous seven awareness techniques.

To be able to identify the energies released by a symbol, it helps to know the issues that the symbol raises. These issues usually provide clues to the energies stored in the symbol.

This technique is based on the spiritual growth principle: *If a dream (or symbol) naturally brings an issue to the surface of awareness, it indicates you have the energies (strength, insight, ability) to begin dealing with that issue.* Thus, if the issue of being a "good girl" surfaced in your dream, communicated by a certain symbol, e.g., the golden mask, what energies would you need to begin to deal with that issue? Those energies are among those presumed to be available to you at this time.

OBJECTIVE:

- to identify some of the energies released by the symbol, in order to translate them into thoughts, actions, and choices in daily life.

*Question to which This Technique Responds:*

What kinds of energies are being released in me by this symbol's appearance?

STEPS:

1. Across the top of a blank piece of paper (or a new page in your dream journal) write the title "Issues and Energies." Then, list the various issues raised by your dream, especially by the chosen symbol. (HINT: In locating the pertinent issues, review earlier techniques, particularly symbol amplification, symbol association, carrying the symbol forward and/or back in time.)

2. Beneath each issue, list the energies or skills you will need to begin dealing successfully with that issue (see page 33). Use more space if you need it.
3. Review this list of energies and skills to help you clarify and identify some of the energies that might be being released in you through this symbol. Note any repeated occurrence of a certain energy or cluster of energies.
4. Mark with an asterisk those energies that you would like to utilize through actions and tasks based on the symbol.

## COMMENT

Here is a list of typical energies released in dream symbols. Do not let this list limit you in any way, but add to it yourself.

| | | | |
|---|---|---|---|
| assertiveness | awareness of God | belonging | courage |
| companionship | cosmic consciousness | creativity | comforting |
| compassion | emotional expression | decisiveness | empathy |
| faith | fortitude (strength) | forgiveness | hope |
| healing | integration | imagination | joy |
| kindness | love | mental energy | meaning |
| nurturing | openness | patience | peace |
| prudence | providing for needs | perseverance | protection |
| purpose | nurturing | receptivity | sensitivity |
| self-esteem | self-affirmation | self-awareness | temperance |
| wisdom | transmitting of life | welcoming | discernment |
| willpower | unconditional love | trust | loyalty |

# ACTION (TASK) TECHNIQUES

The previous eight techniques were designed to bring you to insight and awareness about the issues and energies related to your symbol. They are valuable in that they provide the first level of consciousness, i.e., awareness.

Consciousness, however, is a multi-dimensional experience, and is only completed when insights and awarenesses are translated into appropriate action or self-transformation. Perhaps you are to be changed in some way by the energy of an insight or awareness. Perhaps you or your way of being is to be expanded or transformed.

The following eight symbol techniques are designed to bring you to the level of appropriate action. In other words, the energies released by the symbol need to be brought into action in your daily life by means of tasks related to the symbol. There are three classes of dream tasks:

- *Dreamwork Tasks:* further symbol-work tasks on the chosen symbol that may clarify the energies of that symbol and indicate how and where they might be utilized in daily life (Techniques 9, 10, 11, 12, 13, and 16).
- *Personality Tasks:* reflective tasks that focus on the inner life of the dreamer (Technique 14).
- *Relationship Tasks:* action tasks that focus the symbol energy on the dreamer's outer life, i.e., work, play, relationships (Technique 15).

## Dialogue With the Symbol

This is a very powerful technique that helps establish an in-depth relationship to the symbol. It is to be carried out in solitude and is best written down as it's happening.

OBJECTIVES:

- to befriend the symbol and build an in-depth relationship with it.
- to work with some unanswered questions you have about the symbol.
- to have access to wisdom and insight from the symbol.
- to clarify the meaning and energies released by the symbol.

*Questions to which This Technique Responds:*

Why is this symbol in my dream now? What is it trying to communicate?

STEPS:

1. Prepare a few opening questions to ask the symbol. Depending on the objective you have for the dialogue, your questions may be very specific or general. Some typical opening questions you might ask the symbol:
   - Why did you come into my life now?
   - How are you and I alike? Different?
   - What is your meaning in my life, past, present, future?
   - How are you a part of me?
   - What can I learn from you about actions and choices in my life?
2. Relax and let the symbol come alive in your imagination. Picture yourself present to the symbol. Treat the symbol as if it were a person who could talk to you and answer your questions.
3. Open the dialogue by writing down your first question, and picture yourself asking it of the symbol.
4. Write down whatever response seems to come to you. At first, responses may feel forced, artificial, difficult, made up by you.

Don't let this stop you. All responses are coming from some level of your being. Eventually, the level of response will deepen and what you write will feel more spontaneous, easy-flowing, and natural.

5. Continue writing out the dialogue (i.e., asking questions or responding to questions the symbol may ask you) until the dialogue comes to some resolution or stopping place, as in a normal conversation.
6. Ask a final question or two, such as:
   - Is there anything else I should know or think about?
   - Is there any other symbol with which I should dialogue?
   - Do you have a gift for me?
   - Is there something you want from me?
7. Reread your dialogue, and make note of any insight you have or appropriate action you could take as a result of it.

## COMMENT

Very often a dialogue suggests practical ways that the symbol's energies can be utilized in daily life. It also often opens up new areas to explore, perhaps other symbols to work with.

When the dreamer dialogued with the golden mask, she learned that "*wanting* is good energy to start with." The mask also revealed a number of the benefits it had brought her throughout life as well as the price she had paid for having worn the mask all these years. She also learned that her spiritual growth was not simply a matter of removing her mask and throwing it away, but her task was to maintain some of the mask's qualities, "to develop the opposite of them as well, in order to bring balance into my life."

## SYMBOL TECHNIQUE 10

### Create Expressive Artwork Based on the Symbol

This is an excellent technique for keeping the energies of the symbol alive. Artwork may also be used for meditative purposes. (See Technique 11.)

OBJECTIVES:

- to give the symbol concrete expression and tangible form.
- to keep you conscious of the symbol and its energies by providing something to look at, read, listen to, or refer to.

*Question to which This Technique Responds:*

How can I express the symbol concretely in an art form such as story, song, poetry, drama, music, dance, costume, drawing, painting, collage, or sculpture?

STEPS:

1. Make a list of the different ways you could express the symbol in some art form. For example, with the golden mask, the dreamer could have listed: sculpt the mask from clay; draw it with pencil, crayon or paint; collect photos or paintings of masks; write a poem about the mask; compose a song about the mask; create a fairy tale about the mask. (It does not matter that you feel an amateur with any of these art media; remember, this is an exercise about releasing the energy of a symbol, not a test of your creative talent.)
2. Choose the art form to which you feel most attracted, and set aside some quiet time for the task.
3. When you have collected your materials, instruments or tools for the task, take a few moments to return in imagination to the symbol as it appeared in your dream or waking life experience.
4. When you feel reconnected to the symbol, begin your artwork.
5. When it is complete, reflect on your work and the process it followed, and let yourself feel a sense of completion.

6. Make note of any insights you have about the symbol's energy and how it relates to your daily life.
7. Keep the artwork in some evident place, where you can return to it and be present to it frequently, in order to keep the energies alive.

## COMMENT

The dreamer made a plaster mask which was formed, like the golden mask, to fit her face. In making it she learned that she could control when she wore her mask and when she took it off. As she explained:

> *I realized that the mask's qualities didn't have to be lost, I hold them in my own hands. The mask's qualities could be used, taken off, and put back on at will. I was no longer imprisoned by the mask but neither had I lost its usefulness. I could still be "beautiful" when I wanted to. The mask was still available to me for any of its functions, e.g., hiding, protecting, entertaining, fitting in, which I might choose to utilize.*

## Meditate on the Symbol

This technique is especially appropriate for people who value meditation and do it as a regular spiritual practice in their lives. It also provides a simple, gentle entrance into meditation for those who have never tried it. It is especially satisfying when you have previously done some awareness techniques (e.g., Techniques 3 through 8) on the symbol.

OBJECTIVES:

- to deepen your relationship to the symbol in light of your spiritual growth (to internalize the symbol).
- to nurture and encourage the energies released by the symbol.
- to be quietly in the presence of the symbol.
- to cherish the symbol and call upon its energies for self-transformation.

*Question to which This Technique Responds:*

To what transformation (wholeness, greatness, etc.) does this symbol call me?

STEPS:

1. Set aside 10–30 minutes of undisturbed, quiet time when you can meditate on the symbol.
2. Grow quiet and centered, and meditatively focus on the symbol, using your ordinary method of meditating. For example:
   - You may simply repeat the name of the symbol, or put it into a larger mantra form, e.g., "The golden mask calls me to wholeness."
   - You may re-create the symbol in your imagination (or use your artwork as a focus) and look lovingly and attentively at it as if you were a camera.
   - You may reflect intellectually and emotionally upon the sym-

bol and its meaning in your life, much as you might reflect upon a story or a work of art in a museum.

3. When your meditation period is over, make note of the energies released in you and how they might find appropriate expression in your life.

## COMMENT

The dreamer used her plaster mask as a focus of her attention. She sat with it and held it in her hand. She also held it in front of her face and looked at her "masked appearance" in the mirror.

In her reflections, she was faced with the paradox that the mask was beautiful, but so was her humanness. She felt "encouraged to seek my true humanness."

That the process of integration might be long, difficult, and painful, was clear to her, but she was choosing to "develop within me the masculine energies and integrate them with my feminine energies."

## Research the Symbol

This technique will be particularly enjoyable for those who like to study symbol books and other reference material, or to connect their symbols with fairy tales, mythology, the Bible, or psychological theories. For those who keep dream journals, it also provides a way to research the appearance of the same or similar symbols in earlier dreams. Since this is an enriching experience and not usually a basic symbol technique, do some awareness techniques, such as amplification, before beginning research.

OBJECTIVES:

- to expand, integrate, and confirm your own previous symbol work.
- to connect the dream symbol with earlier dream symbols or with certain archetypal energies.
- to connect with the meaning of the symbol as it is expressed in the culture and community.
- to provide additional avenues for identifying and using the symbol's energy for growth.

*Question to which This Technique Responds:*

What are some of the cultural, historical, and archetypal roots of the symbol?

NOTE:

The research technique may be approached in a variety of ways using different sources and resources; e.g., fairy tales, cultural myths, classical stories, novels, dramas, pieces of music, biblical references, sacred writings, symbol reference works, writings of psychologists who discuss symbols, or your own dream journal.

STEPS:

1. Choose the source or resource you want to use, e.g., fairy tales.

2. Ask yourself an opening question: "What fairy tale (myth, drama, novel, character, piece of music, work of art) does the symbol remind me of? And why?"
3. When you have established a connection between the symbol and, e.g., the fairy tale, ask yourself: "How does this connection speak to me about my current way of being, acting, thinking, choosing, relating?"
4. What energy might that connection be releasing in me and how can I put it to use in my life today?

ALTERNATE STEPS:

The symbol may also be researched by looking it up in a symbol reference book, a biblical concordance, your dream journal, or an index of the collected writings of certain psychologists. For example, the golden mask dreamer looked up the meaning of mask in the writings of psychiatrist Carl Jung.

1. Once you have looked up the reference, take note of the symbol's meanings and (implied) energies given there.
2. Mark those that are a hit for you.
3. Ask yourself: "How does this meaning speak to me about my current way of being, acting, thinking, choosing, relating?"
4. What energies might be released in me and how can I put them to work in my daily life?

SYMBOL TECHNIQUE 13

## Ask Key Questions About the Symbol

The questions in this technique are designed to relate insights about the symbol to your daily life. Remember that once the energies of the symbol are released they need to be transformed into actions and choices about your inner and outer life that may lead to your wholeness and life purpose.

OBJECTIVES:

- to open up additional avenues for using the symbol's energies.
- to relate the symbol's energies to what is going on in your life today.

*Question to which This Technique Responds:*

How else can I explore the symbol and put its energies into action in my life right now?

STEPS:

1. From the list of Key Symbol Questions below, choose those that seem to apply to you.
2. In responding to each of the chosen questions, ask yourself: "How does my response speak to me about my current way of being, acting, thinking, choosing, and relating?"
3. In what way might your response be applied to your life today?

KEY SYMBOL QUESTIONS

1. What are the most important characteristics of the symbol?
2. How am I like the symbol? Qualities and characteristics?
3. How am I unlike the symbol? Qualities and characteristics?
4. What is my major affect (feeling) associated with the symbol?
5. How do the other dream symbols relate to this symbol?

151

6. In the dream, why am I acting toward the symbol the way I'm acting?
7. Would I like to be relating to the symbol in a different way?
8. Why might I need this symbol and its energies now?
9. Does this symbol evoke a question about how I live my life?
10. How is the symbol a gift to me now?
11. Does this symbol occur in my waking life?
12. To what events or experiences do I associate this symbol?

## COMMENT

You may create other key symbol questions that pertain directly to the symbol. For example, after meditating on the story of Daniel and the Lions' Den from the Bible, the dreamer of the golden mask dream was asked by her partner, "How many lions were in the den?" The answer came back spontaneously, "Seven."

When the partner then asked, "What were their names?" it surprised the dreamer, but she immediately began naming the seven lions as Selfish, Greedy, Stingy, Vanity, Hypocrisy, Fear, and Laziness. "I recognized that each of them," said the dreamer, "felt dangerous to the me that was striving for wholeness and holiness. They represented the shadow qualities that I needed to own and deal with. I could also recognize that these huge and powerful beasts contained a lot of energy. I would need to be a special kind of lion tamer to transform such wild, instinctual energy."

## SYMBOL TECHNIQUE 14

### Do Personality Tasks:
### Bring the Symbol's Energies into Your Inner Life

This technique helps complete the cycle of symbol work, from insight to appropriate action. This technique helps specify in task form the energies that have been released by the symbol.

This technique is usually more profitable when done with a partner, a therapist, or a small dream group who know you well. They provide additional alternative suggestions, encouragement, support, and fresh ideas. As a rule, when you choose some personality tasks to do, you make a commitment to your partner(s) to carry out your chosen tasks and to report to them when you have completed your work.

OBJECTIVES:

- to begin applying the symbol's energies to your inner life.
- to keep the energies of the symbol alive in your life.
- to develop do-able tasks that can help transform your personality, nurture your wholeness, and promote your spiritual growth.

*Question to which This Technique Responds:*

How can I use the energies released by the symbol to help transform my personality (inner life)?

STEPS:

1. If you are working with a partner or a group, invite the others to suggest personality tasks you might consider doing. These tasks should relate to the symbol and the energies associated with it.
2. Together, create a written list of 6–10 possible tasks you might do.
3. You choose one or two from the list and agree to carry them out before your next meeting or some specified time. Choose those

tasks at which you are most likely to succeed. Personal transformation succeeds best through a series of small successes.
4. Record your successes and share them with your partner(s).

## COMMENT

In earlier symbol techniques, you were able to specify energies that were being released in you by the symbol and perhaps you even noted areas in your life where you might use that energy.

In this technique you are asked to specify a series of simple tasks that can help focus, use, and nurture those energies for your inner transformation. To qualify as true tasks, the actions chosen must be finite, time-limited, measurable, do-able, and related to the symbol's energies.

Thus, "to list all my good qualities" is not a true task, because it is not finite, not time-limited, not measurable, and probably not do-able to anyone's satisfaction, because you can never know when you have completed the assignment.

However, "to list ten qualities I have that make me a good friend" is finite, time-limited, measurable, do-able task, and one that is related to the symbol's energy. Another appropriate task might be "to recall ten events in my life as examples of each of those ten qualities."

For examples of the ways the golden mask dreamer carried out this technique, see pp. 48–52.

## SYMBOL TECHNIQUE 15

### Do Relationship Tasks:
### Bring the Symbol's Energies into Your Outer Life

Relationship tasks are a natural counterpart to personality tasks. Again, this technique is richest when done with partners or in a small dream group. Let the partners suggest a list of possible tasks that would help you bring the symbol's energies into your outer life—your work, your play, your personal relationships.

OBJECTIVES:

■ to begin applying the symbol's energies to your outer life.
■ to keep the symbol's energies alive.
■ to transform your work, play, and personal relationships.

*Question to which This Technique Responds:*

How can I use the energies released by the symbol to help transform my work, my play, and my personal relationships?

STEPS:

1. If you are working with a partner or a group, invite the others to suggest relationship tasks you might consider doing. These tasks should relate to the symbol and the energies associated with it.
2. Together, create a written list of 6–10 possible tasks you might do.
3. You choose one or two from the list, and agree to carry them out before your next meeting or some specified time. Choose those tasks at which you are most likely to succeed.
4. Record your successes and share them with your partner(s).

COMMENT

Be sure to develop tasks that are finite, time-limited, measurable, do-able, and related to the symbol's energy. Thus, "to be kinder to people than I used to be" is not a true task, since it is not time-limited, measurable, and you can never know when you have completed the task. Better to select a task, such as "to do one small act of kindness or generosity each day for a week." This task is finite, time-limited, measurable, do-able and, for the mask dreamer, related directly to the symbol's energy. This technique also provides a specific opportunity for consciously choosing to act on the dream symbol's energy.

You can continue doing personality tasks and relationship tasks for years, or as long as it takes to complete your self-transformation. As long as you keep exercising the symbol's energies, those energies will keep flowing. The golden mask dreamer has been working from the energies of her dream for well over ten years, and she reports that the energies are still strong.

Look for Dreams That Give Guidance and Confirmation

It's always nice to know that the symbol work you're doing is on the right track. In this technique, you ask your dreams to give you such confirmation and to guide you to the next step of your spiritual growth.

OBJECTIVE:

■ to find in subsequent dreams guidance and confirmation that the symbol work you're doing is leading you in the right direction, the direction of your growth in consciousness and wholeness.

*Questions to which This Technique Responds:*

How can I use my dreams to tell me if I am on the right track? Do my dreams tell me where to go from here?

STEPS:

1. To use this technique, you may either observe whatever dreams come to you following a major dream, or you may suggest to yourself before falling asleep that you will receive a dream of guidance and/or confirmation of your symbol work.
2. When you awake, record your dream and treat it as a "commentary" on how you are using the energies released by the original symbol. (The new dream may refer to your thoughts, actions, choices, personal relationships, work, play, and chosen dream tasks.)
3. Choose major symbols from such guidance dreams (using Techniques 1 and 2) and do basic symbol work with them, to clarify issues and energies.

COMMENT

For the golden mask dreamer, this technique became very important. Her confirming and guidance dreams refined the self-transformation work she had begun and clarified the energies that were most readily available to her.

If This Were My Dream . . .

This interactive dreamwork technique, which may also be applied to symbol work, was developed by Montague Ullman in his book *Working With Dreams* (Delacorte, New York, 1979). It is widely used in dreamwork groups because it is simple, enjoyable, and gets everyone involved in each dream that is shared. This technique presumes you are working in a dream group or with a dreamwork partner.

OBJECTIVE:

- to find new meanings for your symbol and new avenues for symbol work in the meanings triggered by your symbol in others.

*Question to which This Technique Responds:*

If this were my dream, what would the symbol mean to me?

STEPS:

1. If you have not yet told your dream, tell it to the group and then tell them the symbol on which you are focused.
2. In turn, each of the others in the group then responds to your dream symbol by saying, "If this were my dream, that symbol would mean to me. . . ." Each respondent then talks about the symbol and what it might signify in his or her own life. (The invitation is *not* for them to make interpretations for the dreamer, but simply to treat the dream and symbol as if it were their own and find wisdom for themselves in it. If the dreamer resonates to any of their observations, it is a gift to the dreamer.)
3. After hearing all the respondents' insights about the symbol, you, the dreamer, may tell the group which ones were helpful and how they helped. (You may want to take notes during this process or use a tape recorder.)

COMMENT

In this technique, the universal language of the symbol is honored, each member of the dream group feels personally involved, and the dreamer gets the benefit of hearing many meanings reflected in his or her dream symbol. The dreamer receives a variety of perceptions of the symbol and is free to take wisdom from any and all of them.

This last technique clearly honors the idea that a dream is also a gift to the entire community. This idea was expressed in early biblical times and, according to anthropologists, is still honored in numerous cultures today. Accordingly, this technique helps build community through sharing, openness, cooperation, supportive interaction, valuing of each other's spiritual seeking, and the totally unique contribution of each participant.

# SUMMARY

## Awareness Techniques

1. Identify Symbols in a Dream Report
2. Choose a Symbol on Which to Focus
3. Get Immersed in the Symbol
4. Amplify the Symbol
5. Carry the Symbol Forward in Time
6. Carry the Symbol Backward in Time
7. Associate to the Symbol
8. Name Some Energies Released by the Symbol

## Action (Task) Techniques

9. Dialogue with the Symbol
10. Create Expressive Artwork Based on the Symbol
11. Meditate on the Symbol
12. Research the Symbol
13. Ask Key Questions About the Symbol
14. Do Personality Tasks: Bring the Symbol's Energies into Your Inner Life
15. Do Relationship Tasks: Bring the Symbol's Energies into Your Outer Life
16. Look for Dreams that Give Guidance and Confirmation
17. If This Were My Dream . . .

# AFTERWORD

When my 50th birthday was approaching, a Jewish friend of mine told me that in their religious tradition during the 50th year people were obliged to free their slaves. I saw that act of liberation as a wonderful metaphor for what I wanted my 50th birthday to be. So I invited many friends to my home for my birthday party and asked them to celebrate with me the freeing of myself from the slavery of fear and dysfunctional beliefs, and from the bondage of insecurity and the need for approval. In their presence, I declared myself free. Since that day, part of my daily meditation has been to choose freedom.

In preparing the manuscript for this book and reviewing all the symbol work I had done on the child in the golden mask, I came to discover another dimension of me that needed to be set free. The child in the mask was angry. I needed to acknowledge that fact as something positive. I needed to take ownership of my own justifiable anger, not just of my ability to be assertive, and I wanted to use its energies constructively in my life and in the world.

As a good little girl, I was told I must not be angry. Anger was a sin, and a capital one at that. My church–and many New Age religions as well—recommend doing away with angry feelings, replacing them with love, or at least not allowing them to be a part of you. However, the woman I am today and the world in general need to accept and find constructive ways for using the energy of justifiable anger. Too many injustices are being allowed to exist unrestricted, too many rapes of the ecology and of the human spirit are allowed to happen because we don't know how to own and use our justifiable anger. In my dream, the child was angry, and rightly so, because it had been forgotten and deprived of nourishment. Its rights as a human being had been neglected. I need that child's anger today to acknowledge and cry out against the injustices of which I am aware, and injustice wherever I see it.

When I was a child, my mother told me I had a horrible temper,

161

that I must get rid of it, and that I should be punished for having it. She shamed me out of my right to be angry at the injustices of my childhood. What a crime against me, that my justifiable anger had been shamed and punished. What a crime against humanity when anger at greed, crime, exploitation, and rape of all kinds is shamed and punished.

Edmund Burke, the statesman, said, "The only thing necessary for the triumph of evil is for good people to do nothing." We need our righteous anger to cry out for the needs of all God's creatures and creation itself. We need to be able to make ourselves heard or else, like the child in the golden mask, we risk the slow death and starvation of our human spirits.

Instead of purging myself of anger, as my mother and my early religious upbringing would have me do, I must take ownership of that tremendous and precious energy and make responsible use of it.

# RECOMMENDED READING

Caligor, Leopold, and May, Rollo, *Dreams and Symbols—Man's Unconscious Language,* Basic Books, New York, 1968.

Caprio, Betsy, and Hedberg, Thomas, *In a Dream Workshop,* Paulist Press, New York, 1987.

Chetwynd, Tom, *How to Interpret Your Own Dreams (In One Minute or Less), An Encyclopedic Dictionary,* Bell Publishing, New York, 1972.

Cirlot, J.E., *A Dictionary of Symbols,* Philosophical Library, New York, 1962.

Cooper, J.C., *An Illustrated Encyclopedia of Traditional Symbols,* Thames & Hudson, London, 1978.

Davis, Alan, *What Your Dreams Mean* (A Dream Dictionary), Bantam, New York, 1969.

Fliess, Robert, *Symbol, Dream, and Psychosis* (Freudian), International Universities Press, New York, 1974.

French, Thomas, and Fromm, Erika, *Dream Interpretation—A New Approach* (Freudian), Basic Books, New York, 1964.

Gendlin, Eugene, *Let Your Body Interpret Your Dreams,* Chiron Publications, Wilmette, IL, 1986.

Guthiel, Emil, *The Handbook of Dream Analysis,* Washington Square Press, New York, 1967.

Hall, Calvin, and Nordby, Vernon, *A Primer of Jungian Psychology,* New American Library, New York, 1973.

Jung, C.G., *Man and His Symbols,* Doubleday, Garden City, 1964.

Mattoon, Mary, *Applied Dream Analysis: A Jungian Approach,* Winston Wiley, Washington, 1978.

O'Connor, Peter, *Dreams and the Search for Meaning,* Paulist Press, New York, 1986.

Sanford, John, *Dreams and Healing,* Paulist Press, New York, 1978.

Sanford, John, *Invisible Partners,* Paulist Press, New York, 1980.

Savary, Louis, Berne, Patricia, and Williams, Strephon, *Dreams and Spiritual Growth,* Paulist Press, New York, 1984.

Taylor, Jeremy, *Dream Work: Techniques for Discovering the Creative Power in Dreams,* Paulist Press, New York, 1983.

Ullman, Montague, and Zimmerman, Nan, *Working With Dreams,* Delacorte, New York, 1979.

Watkins, Mary, *Waking Dreams,* Harper, New York, 1977.

Williams, Strephon Kaplan, *Jungian-Senoi Dreamwork Manual,* Journey Press, Berkeley, 1984.